NEW TESTAMENT MESSAGE

A Biblical-Theological Commentary

Wilfrid Harrington, O.P. and Donald Senior, C.P.

EDITORS

New Testament Message, Volume 17

THE
PASTORAL
EPISTLES

Robert J. Karris, O.F.M.

Michael Glazier, Inc.
Wilmington, Delaware

MICHAEL GLAZIER, INC.
1210A King Street
Wilmington, Delaware 19801

Library of Congress Catalog Card Number: 79-52925
International Standard Book Number
New Testament Message series: 0-89453-123-9
THE PASTORAL EPISTLES: 0-89453-140-9

Printed in the United States of America by Abbey Press

Contents

EDITORS' PREFACE

New Testament Message is a commentary series designed
to bring the best of biblical scholarship to a wide audience.
Anyone who is sensitive to the mood of the church today is
aware of a deep craving for the Word of God. This interest
in reading and praying the scriptures is not confined to a
religious elite. The desire to strengthen one's faith and to
mature in prayer has brought Christians of all types and all
ages to discover the beauty of the biblical message. Our age
has also been heir to an avalanche of biblical scholarship.
Recent archaeological finds, new manuscript evidence, and
the increasing volume of specialized studies on the Bible
have made possible a much more profound penetration of
the biblical message. But the flood of information and its
technical nature keeps much of this scholarship out of the
hands of the Christian who is eager to learn but is not a
specialist. *New Testament Message* is a response to this
need.

The subtitle of the series is significant: "A Biblical-
Theological Commentary." Each volume in the series, while
drawing on up-to-date scholarship, concentrates on bring-
ing to the fore in understandable terms the specific message of each biblical author. The essay-format (rather than
a word-by-word commentary) helps the reader savor the
beauty and power of the biblical message and, at the same
time, understand the sensitive task of responsible biblical
interpretation.

A distinctive feature of the series is the amount of space
given to the "neglected" New Testament writings, such as
Colossians, James, Jude, the Pastoral Letters, the Letters

of Peter and John. These briefer biblical books make a significant but often overlooked contribution to the richness of the New Testament. By assigning larger than normal coverage to these books, the series hopes to give these parts of Scripture the attention they deserve.

Because *New Testament Message* is aimed at the entire English speaking world, it is a collaborative effort of international proportions. The twenty-two contributors represent biblical scholarship in North America, Britain, Ireland and Australia. Each of the contributors is a recognized expert in his or her field, has published widely, and has been chosen because of a proven ability to communicate at a popular level. And, while all of the contributors are Roman Catholic, their work is addressed to the Christian community as a whole. The New Testament is the patrimony of all Christians. It is the hope of all concerned with this series that it will bring a fuller appreciation of God's saving Word to his people.

Wilfrid Harrington, O.P.
Donald Senior, C.P.

In gratitude to my
Franciscan brothers,
past and present,

who so generously
form, support, and love me.

GENERAL INTRODUCTION
TO THE PASTORALS

The Pastorals and I

LET ME BEGIN by sharing my "love story" with the Pastorals. My courtship with them began some ten years ago when I concentrated all my efforts on them for my doctoral dissertation at Harvard Divinity School. Over the years our relationship has been hot and cold. Four years of deep sharing led me to two false conclusions: 1) I thought I knew what they were all about; 2) it was impossible to live with their imperfections. During the next five years I virtually neglected them. But then I turned forty. We're together again. This past year my eyes have been opened wide to their beauty, depth, brilliance, and relevance for contemporary church life. I have fallen in love with them at a much deeper level than before. I see their flawed nature and incompleteness against the background of their beauty and appreciate them much more because these weaknesses make them so human and real.

As I mentioned, the one factor that has contributed most to my appreciation of the Pastorals lies within my own life story—this past year I turned forty. One of the great joys and thrills of turning forty is undertaking the transition from being a young man to being a middle-aged man. The joys, the questionings, the breast-beatings, the re-commitments, the grateful assessment of the past, the probing of the future, all of these are part of a transition in one's life.

They have helped me appreciate the Pastorals as documents which come from a church in transition. My life experience has opened my eyes, my mind, my heart to capture the beauty and imperfection of the Christians who stand behind the Pastorals. They are people undergoing the transition from the apostolic age to the post-apostolic age. They are questioning what they should take from the past as they move towards the future. They are weak and have made mistakes. They are re-committing themselves to Jesus and to Paul in a new age. They are struggling against those who tell them that the world is evil and to be shunned.

If we move from this forty-year old's experience of transition, we can find a more general analogy by which to appreciate the Pastorals. That analogy is the contemporary experience of millions of Roman Catholics who live in the transition from a pre-Vatican II church to a post-Vatican II church. The transition period lasts for decades. There is uncertainty, the letting-go of the "siege mentality," the joy and anxiety of searching for models and heroes, visions projected and in the process of being realized, prophets whose voices are finally heard and those whose voices sound on deaf ears.

Yes, the personal and communal experience of transition can help us appreciate what the Pastorals are about. In what follows, I develop the model of the Pastorals as documents addressing themselves to questions of transition. In the Introduction to 2 Tim. I will develop a further aspect of transition, the experience of loss.

The Pastorals Guide
Churches in the Process of Transition

A. The Pastorals are Pseudonymous Writings

The Pastorals are not written by Paul, but by someone else in his name. It is not easy for us moderns to grasp this concept of pseudonymous writings. And that for two reasons. First, we are raised on an ethical view of writing.

The writing is either by the author whose name appears on the cover or else it is plagiarism. And plagiarism is punishable by law. Of course, this either-or falters on the admission that some authors use pen-names, for example, Mark Twain. The second reason is closely parallel to the first. We have a tendency to absolutize our way of viewing or doing things. In other words, we have a hard time thinking ourselves out of our contemporary experience into a period when they did not have electricity, running water, or did not publish books the way we do. It's the difficulty we have when we travel through a foreign country and find ourselves constantly saying: "Back home we do things differently." But this isn't back home.

I am helped to appreciate the pseudonymous nature of the Pastorals when I recall that there are letters dating from the time of the Pastorals which purport to be written by Socrates. They were written in Socrates' spirit to say what he would have if he were alive at that time. I am helped by contemporary scholarly views of the gospels which maintain that some of the sayings of Jesus did not come from him, but were created by the primitive church to solve its problems in his spirit. I am helped by the example a Coptic priest, Father Michael Tafesse, shared with me. He had received a letter from the thousand-year-old monastery of Dabralibanos, signed with the name of its founder. It is obvious that this group of monks knew that their founder had been deceased for some 1000 years, yet they wrote in his name and signed his name to the letter. These good monks were not lying. I am helped by what recent Vatican documents say about the interpretation of Scripture. We must interpret the Scriptures in accordance with the literary forms of their times. And the writing of pseudonymous letters was a literary form at the time of the Pastorals.

Difficult as it may be, do not let the strangeness of this concept of pseudonymous writing put you off from appreciating the beauty of the Pastorals.

B. The Time and Occasion of the Pastorals

These letters of transition were all written at the same time, namely, around A.D. 110. They were written at a time when the first wave of official persecution under Domitian (A.D. 96) had washed ashore and was still causing repercussions in sporadic persecutions in Asia Minor (cf. Ignatius of Antioch and Pliny's Letter to Trajan). They were written when the Pauline letters were being collected in various Pauline centers. They were written at a time when gnostics claimed that Paul supported their world-hating positions. They were written when communities were moving from the position of a small, isolated sect to that of a universal church, which exists in a pluralistic world, embracing the good things of the cultures around them, supporting civic and governmental goals, fostering good citizenship.

C. Means of Transition

The author's main means of effecting the transition from an apostolic time to a post-apostolic church is *the image of Paul.* Paul is *the* apostle for the churches in transition; he, not the Twelve, is the font of the traditions found in the Pastorals. He is the suffering apostle and martyr. His suffering and death interpret the creeds and hymnic materials in the Pastorals. His example instills encouragement in those Christians who suffer for the gospel in a persecution-prone situation. Paul is the greatest sinner, and that image gives comfort to new Christians joining the Pauline communities. Paul lends his apostolic authority to the exhortations for daily life in 1 Tim and Titus. Through these exhortations Christianity walks hand in hand with the best secular ethics of its day. Paul is the one who combats heresy by what he teaches and especially by his life of martyrdom for the sake of the gospel. The gospel Paul preaches is not just for an elite few, but for all people. The gospel Paul preaches projects God as a loving creator. Against the gnostics Paul champions the goodness of creation and of marriage. In brief, the author remembers Paul the way he does in order to project a vision for churches in transition. Walking in the footsteps of this Paul, these churches will successfully move into a new era of Christian existence.

The author of the Pastorals knows full well that there is no transition without *structure*. The past does not flow into the future willy-nilly; these must be structure. And so there is to be structure in the churches undergoing transition, for example, a college of elders, or a bishop. But the author is flexible, for he allows for different structures as long as there is structure.

The author insists upon *sound teaching*. In combat with the gnostic heretics and in search of continuity with the Pauline tradition, the author stresses teaching which promotes health and soundness within the Christian community. The "sound teaching" or "the deposit of faith" or the "sure sayings" are not, however, to be viewed as something static. As we will have frequent occasion to note in the commentary, the church leaders who provide the structure for the church in transition are to develop the "sound teaching" by applying it ever again to new situations. And such applications and development will reveal ever new facets of the deposit of faith.

The author of the Pastorals is eminently *practical*. In the pressure of transition the author has little time for speculation which does not lead to improvement in conduct. A mere recollection of the sound doctrine will not effect transition. The sound doctrine has to be remembered in the performance of good deeds. The author clearly is in favor of the principle: "By their fruits you shall know them."

Christians who participate in the transition must be marked by *irreproachable conduct*. Their conduct should show to non-Christians that Christianity is not inimical to the goals of society. Christians are good citizens.

Finally, *flexibility* is the by-word of transition. The author borrows from many Greco-Roman exhortatory traditions and gives multiple guidance for his churches in transition. He does not insist on one, and only one, structure. When he sees the need for an institution which his surrounding culture does not have, he creates a new one— the order of widows. He adapts Paul's teaching of justification by faith to meet his changed circumstances when "works of the Law" was no longer an issue.

Such are the means of transition. In the next section we overlap some of them as we discuss the theology which makes transition possible.

D. *Theology of Transition*

The author's teaching about God is the heart of what he has to say about transition. By accentuating God as Creator and Sovereign, he is able to attack his gnostic opponents who deny the goodness of creation. By means of his view of God as all-good and creator he is empowered to build upon Paul's use of secular ethics (see Phil 4:8) and to derive exhortations for his churches from the best models of secular ethics available to him.

An added feature of this underlining of God the creator and sovereign is the author's "low Christology," that is, Christology which does not emphasize the divinity of Jesus Christ. Against the gnostics who would deny the goodness of matter, the author highlights the humanity of Jesus Christ. Because God chose to appear in the man Christ Jesus, those who follow in Jesus' footsteps must not abandon the world, but involve themselves in creation and in those institutions which nurture human life.

The author teaches that churches which are successful in transition devote themselves to God in prayer and liturgy. But not any liturgy. It must be liturgy which enables practical Christian life. The Christian whose reciting of the creed leads to good conduct knows what the creed is all about. "Good deeds" are proof that the church is on the right road of transition.

Theocentricism, creation theology, low Christology, orthopraxis, these are the theological keys of transition. And they are important keys. But in fashioning them, the author had to neglect other important theological factors. First, a theology of the Holy Spirit does not seem to be the author's forte. Working from his theological principles, the author does not see fit to develop Paul's theology of the Spirit beyond a discussion of the charism of church leaders. He does not have much space within his theological system of transition to ponder the implications of Paul's words, "Now the Lord is the Spirit, and where the Spirit of the Lord is, there is freedom" (2 Cor 3:17) or "If we live by the Spirit, let us also walk by the Spirit" (Gal 5:25).

Another weakness of the author's theology of transition is the black-and-white picture he paints of his gnostic opponents. Unlike the gnostics, the author does not address himself to the problem of evil. The gnostics came to theological grips with this problem and opted out of the world as a solution. The author of the Pastorals affirms the goodness of creation and of human institutions and exhorts his churches to go into and to be at home in the world. But he softpedals the gnostic critique of a world-affirming theology. Christians, brought up on the theology of the Pastorals, will celebrate human and Christian life, but must look elsewhere for an appreciation of the problem of evil in the world.

If I might return to the image of "love story" with which I opened this Introduction, I would say that the Pastorals have the blemishes of a skimpy theology of the Holy Spirit and a too-enthusiastic theology of creation. At one time these flaws turned me off, but now I see them against the background of the Pastorals' beauty. These blemishes pale in comparison with a theology which gives top billing to a human Savior and to involvement in God's good creation. Besides, the Pastorals and I know that ours is not such an exclusive relationship that it leaves no room for friendships with others in the New Testament who will complement our weaknesses and strengths.

Contemporary Relevance of the Pastorals

To continue the image of my "love story" with the Pastorals, I must admit that when I returned to the Pastorals to write this commentary, I thought that I knew what they were all about. How wrong I was! They have taught me much about church life and about human life.

The Pastorals have many things to tell us who are experiencing the transition from a pre-Vatican II to a post-Vatican II church. They tell us of the importance of fidelity. If the churches of the Pastorals had moved into the post-apostolic age and had not been faithful to the gospel, they would have lost their souls in the process. But as we will have ample opportunity to note in the commentary, fidelity does not mean rigidity. The author of the Pastorals does not bury the talents of the Pauline tradition in the earth until the storms of transition have passed. He courageously moves into new times and changed circumstances with the Pauline deposit. And he finds that his courageous faith and hope are rewarded by the blossoming of that deposit. He is not afraid of scientific and cultural developments in the world around him, but embraces what is good within them for his churches. "We've never done it before" is not a principle in his vocabulary of transition. He can fight against the flood of his culture and create an institution which is in accord with his faith and vision—the order of widows. The threat of persecution does not keep him off the streets of the world. He flees from a ghetto mentality and highlights a universal mission in accordance with the will of a God who desires the salvation of all.

When I renewed my acquaintance with the Pastorals, I suspected that I would be enamored of what they had to say about church life. But I never dreamt that they would teach me so much about the values of ordinariness and of human existence. 1 Tim and Titus are replete with exhortations about the ordinary things of life, such as how to relate to one's spouse. That the author insists on fidelity amidst the humdrum activities of daily life may not be so startling.

What is startling is that he infers these duties from the fact that Christ Jesus, our Savior, appeared in human history as a human being. Our salvation lies in the ordinariness of our fidelity to those commitments which make up our daily lives.

The Pastorals are a strong antidote to one of the greatest temptations all of us have. That is the temptation to flee away from our humanness. This temptation to find eternal beauty or the fountain of youth is made even more seductive these days by our consumer culture. Youth is king. We remove the wrinkles and weakness of old age from our sight into old age colonies and nursing homes. We decorate up the dead lest they remind us of our own transitoriness. Grey hair is a touch of death. Psychiatrists will fix us, so that the human condition of doubt, anxiety, and depression will evaporate. The Pastorals force you and me to reflect upon our humanness, a humanness in which God our Savior appeared, a humanness in which we prove our day-in-and-day-out fidelity to God and our fellow human beings. Salvation is not to be found in withdrawal from our human condition. The Christian sucks deeply at the marrow of life.

The Pastorals have indeed stolen my heart. This forty year old will never be the same. At the feet of the Pastorals I have rediscovered the beauty of ordinary things which prove my love—daily. I am captivated by the mystery and beauty of being human. I continue to develop the laugh wrinkles around my eyes, for there is so much in life to celebrate.

My Goal in This Commentary

I have talked about the Pastorals as documents for churches undergoing transition. I have discussed their weaknesses and strengths. Now I pause to make explicit what has been implicit in much of what I have said so far in this Introduction. My goal in this commentary is to be positive and pastoral.

Let me make my point by an anecdote. Last fall my work took me to Notre Dame. On the campus of St. Mary's there is a road which leads through some of the most spectacular fall foliage I have ever seen. While I was walking down this road, contemplating the beauty of each tree, one tree enraptured me. Its reds were indescribably beautiful. As I studied the various parts of the tree to appreciate its beauty more deeply, I realized that one-third of the tree was stripped of all sign of life. I looked at that spent third for some time. When my gaze returned to the entire tree, the spent third faded out of my sight. The brilliantly alive parts of the tree held my attention.

In this commentary my eye is for life. I accentuate the positive. Like a conductor, I strive to interpret the musical score of the Pastorals so that their vision of God's revelation might light a path for your life. May you come to know the joys of their friendship.

Acknowledgments

One of the joys of our human condition is that a book like this is a cooperative venture. I am filled with deep gratitude as I recall and acknowledge the insights generated by Jacinta Van Winkel, Paul Davidson, and Michael Tafesse during our M.A. seminar on the Pastorals the Spring of 1978. I am very grateful for the work of and conversations with Jerome Quinn and Luke Johnson of this country and for the work of Norbert Brox and Peter Trummer of West Germany. On the home front, I express much gratitude to Ms. Shirley Brin for her splendid and expert preparation of this manuscript for publication. Finally, I acknowledge the support and encouragement my Franciscan community at Catholic Theological Union has shown me over the years and especially during the writing of this book.

2 Timothy

INTRODUCTION TO 2 TIMOTHY -
THE IMAGE OF LOSS:
PAUL IS DEAD

BEFORE DISCUSSING loss as my means of imaging 2 Tim, I should answer a question which may be troubling you: Why am I treating 2 Tim before 1 Tim? There are a number of reasons. First, the canonical order of 1 Tim, 2 Tim, and Titus is not sacrosanct and is based on the mere length of the letters (six chapters, four chapters, three chapters). Second, since the Pastoral Epistles were all written at the same time, there is no reason for thinking that the author wanted 1 Tim read before 2 Tim. Third, there's the practical consideration that the data in 1 Tim and Titus are so similar that they are better commented on back to back, with 2 Tim given a separate discussion. Fourth and most importantly, I treat 2 Tim first because of its great emphasis on the person and image of Paul. In 1 Tim and Titus this image will recur, with somewhat diminished emphasis, and is the means by which the author interprets his traditional materials of regulations and creeds. By commenting on 2 Tim first, I will highlight the various dimensions of the author's image of Paul and thus prepare us for the repetition and development of those dimensions in 1 Tim and Titus.

What image do you have of the Pastorals? What image do they project? That of a church frightened of heresy, insistent upon law and order, taking to the highways of the future with the deposit of faith fearfully clutched to its bosom? The Pastorals have been read in this light. Their image is definitely not that of happy and carefree times when family and friends are gathered for the holidays.

Yes, it must be admitted that the image projected by the Pastorals is sober and somewhat somber. But that image is not negative. I suggest that the somber image projected by the Pastorals be specified as that of the pain, stumbling, and transition of loss. Paul is dead. What is the church to do?

Let me go behind the scenes of this image of loss by sharing two examples of loss with you. One is the loss of a loved one; the other is the loss of a hero.

At a time of loss the feeling of loneliness is more painful than any persecutor's rack. You struggle to cope. You hear a strong voice inside you encouraging you to show "them," whoever they may be, that you can survive the loss. During a time of loss you stick to the tried and true ways of doing things. It is not a time for innovation. It's a time for memories rather than plans for the future. It is a time to gather mementoes and remembrances. People say, "Let me take that to remember her by." People eulogize the departed one by saying, "Let's imitate her joyous way of showing hospitality." And paradoxically, the beloved is sometimes more present in death than in life.

Some months or years after the loss of the beloved, the innovating tendency returns to the bereaved. And often-times innovations are seen as interpretations of the mind of the lost one. "My wife would have wanted me to remarry." "Dad wouldn't have minded us selling the family homestead. He was always great in adapting to new circumstances."

Moving from the loss of a loved one, I share with you my experience of losing a hero, someone who was a powerful influence in my life and school. Some years back Father Geron Fournelle, O.F.M., the chairperson of the Bible Department at Catholic Theological Union, died suddenly. It was near the end of the school year. I felt his loss keenly and wondered how the school, the department, and I would continue without him. His mantle of leadership fell on my shoulders as I was elected departmental chairperson. In the aftermath of his loss, I retained his tried and true policies about equivalencies, course offerings, etc. In my dealings in the department and with others I determined to continue the memory of his kindness and wisdom. "They" were counting on me, and I would not let them down. With the passing of time and with the rapid evolution of the school I had to innovate and to adapt old policies to new circumstances, saying to myself as I did so that my hero would have done the same if he were alive.

What do these examples tell us about the image projected by the Pastorals? They show us the richness of the image of loss. The Pastorals presuppose that Paul, their beloved apostle and hero, is dead. How should the church cope with that loss? The church copes by adhering to the tried and true regulations for bishops and others which are so much in evidence in 1 Tim and Titus. The church remembers Paul and models its life on his, especially on his steadfastness during suffering. The church shows "them," whoever these opponents may be, that it can persevere despite the loss of Paul.

On the one hand, then, the Pastorals convey the image of a church which has just experienced the loss of its apostle and hero, Paul. But if we dig just a bit below the surface of the Pastorals, we see a church which has creatively adapted the life of Paul and his teachings for its own changed circumstances. For example, the Paul, who from time to time told individual churches to imitate him (see, e.g., 1 Cor 11:1), now is the model for all Christians to imitate.

To recapitulate, I suggest that the image to hold in mind while reading 2 Tim—and also 1 Tim and Titus—is that of the loss of a loved one, the loss of a hero. This image will allow us to see the contemporary value of the Pastorals more clearly and readily than the images of epistles which champion ecclesiastical law and order or of an author who takes the major risk of his day by getting out of bed in the morning. The key to this image of loss is *memory*. The way Paul is remembered in the Pastorals tells us about the author's values and about his dreams for the future of the church.

PAUL IS THE APOSTLE FOR THE CHURCHES.
2 Tim 1:1-2.

> **1** Paul, an apostle of Christ Jesus by the will of God according to the promise of the life which is in Christ Jesus,
> ²To Timothy, my beloved child:
> Grace, mercy, and peace from God the Father and Christ Jesus our Lord.

This preface is a building block in the construction of the image of Paul. Paul is *the* apostle for the churches. He did not receive his apostleship from human authority. God has willed and called him to be an apostle. And Paul's apostolic charge is to proclaim that God's promise of life has been fulfilled in the coming of Christ Jesus (see the commentary on Titus 1:1-4 for more detail on the relationship between Jesus Christ and hope).

"My beloved child" (1:1) echoes two passages in Paul's genuine epistles and reveals the bonds of love that tied Paul to Timothy: "Therefore I sent to you Timothy, my beloved and faithful child in the Lord, to remind you of my ways in Christ, as I teach them everywhere in every church" (1 Cor 4:17); "I hope in the Lord Jesus to send Timothy to you soon, so that I may be cheered by news of you. I have no one like him, who will be genuinely anxious for your welfare. They all look after their own interests, not those of Jesus Christ. But Timothy's worth you know, how as a son with a father he has served with me in the gospel" (Phil 2:19-22).

But if Timothy is so dear to Paul, why does the author address Timothy so formally and as if they had never met before: "Paul, an apostle of Christ Jesus by the will of God . . ."? It would be like me writing a letter to a dear friend or, better yet, to my mother and beginning: "Robert J.

Karris, by the grace of God a priest of the Roman Catholic Church, by personal endeavor a doctor of theology, for the purpose of preaching the Word of God, to my dear and beloved Mother: Blessings, much peace and love." Mom would immediately be suspicious and would wonder what I was up to. What is our author up to? With the very first words of 2 Tim our author is busily painting his images of Paul and Timothy. Paul, as we have seen, is *the* apostle. His words, and especially his example, are weighty and precious. Timothy, as someone close and dear to Paul, is a trustworthy conveyer of the meaning of Paul's life and teachings to a generation living in changed circumstances. Seen from another perspective, 2 Tim and the Pastorals in general are not addressed solely to Timothy or church leaders like him, but to the church at large. The church is exhorted to imitate Paul and Timothy and to pass on to new generations what these heroes have taught.

At this point in the commentary I pause to answer two important questions connected with 2 Tim 1:1-2: What kind of letter if 2 Tim? How is the formula "in Christ Jesus" used in the Pastorals?

What Kind of Letter is 2 Timothy?

If you're like me, the predominant image you have of a letter is a "letter home" or a "letter to a friend." But upon further reflection I realize that the letter carrier may also bring me letters of sympathy, letters of advertisement, fan mail, business letters, letters of acceptance or rejection, etc. From my reading of newspapers and magazines I know of letters to the editor and open letters. When we receive a letter which is not the typical "letter from a friend," we can easily misinterpret it if we don't switch the gears of our reading. Usually something in the letter will tip us off and tell us how to read it, so that, for example, we don't read a summons for jury duty as an appeal to contribute to a judge's campaign for re-election.

Believe it or not, in antiquity there were at least as many different types of letters as there are today. One letter theorist (Pseudo-Demetrius) lists twenty-one different types of letters. Another (Pseudo-Libanius) mentions forty-one different letter styles. Into what category does 2 Tim fall? 2 Tim is closest to a personal paraenetic or exhortatory letter. In this type of letter people are exhorted to follow good personal example rather than to follow mere abstract norms. In letters of this type memory is vitally important. Here are relevant paragraphs from *Isocrates to Demonicus*, in which Isocrates exhorts Demonicus to imitate his father. I have italicized the key words:

> So then, since I deem it fitting that those who strive for distinction and are ambitious for education should *emulate the good* and not the bad, I have dispatched to you this discourse . . . . Nay, if you will but *recall* also your father's principles, you will have from your own house a *noble example* of what I am telling you . . . . For the present, however, I have produced a sample of the nature of your father Hipponicus, *after whom you should pattern your life as after an example*, regarding his conduct as your law, and striving *to imitate* and emulate your father's virtue . . . (paragraphs 2, 9, and 11; Loeb translation modified).

Surely, this example from an ancient document seems foreign to our everyday experience. Our mail boxes may be stuffed with junk mail, but not with personal paraenetic letters. Imagine, then, my surprise when I recalled that I had recently received such a letter. It was a letter from my Provincial, or religious superior, addressed to me and all Franciscans under his jurisdiction. I quote the salient portions of this paraenetic letter, italicizing key phrases:

> Now, in our fervent commitment to the ministry of justice and peace, I think we can see more forcefully and clearly than ever before the deep need we have to be true Franciscan contemplatives in our approach to every aspect of our Franciscan lives. Otherwise, we run the

risk of becoming *activist do-gooders* instead of men of the Gospel on fire with the Seraphic spirit that *Francis of Assisi has willed for us*. If we want *a concrete example and model of this spirit*, we need only peruse the pages of *Down and Out*, the pamphlet on *Fr. Berard Scarborough* recently published by the Franciscan Vocation Center. Berard made the same commitment to the Franciscan life that we have made, and, in him, the ideal of contemplation closely united with service to the poor came alive! May his *example* inspire us to keep growing towards the realization of this ideal in our own lives.

In this exhortatory letter the author challenges his readers to remember the examples of St. Francis of Assisi, their founder, and more recently, of Fr. Berard Scarborough. If they don't follow these examples, they'll become "activist do-gooders." Allowing for changes in circumstances, one could compare this letter to 2 Tim. I would substitute Paul for Francis of Assisi, Timothy for Fr. Berard, and "those who have swerved from the truth" (2 Tim 2:18) for "activist do-gooders." The names have been changed, but the scheme is the same.

But you do not have to be a Demonicus or a Karris to experience a personal paraenetic letter. Listen carefully the next time a letter from the bishop is read in church on Sunday. In exhorting you, for example, to enter into the spirit of Advent, he challenges you to recall and imitate John the Baptist's readiness for the Lord and not to imitate those who immerse themselves so deeply in the consumerism of Christmas shopping that they cannot hear the voice of the Lord in their lives. The scenario of a personal paraenetic letter is present: memory, imitation, the example of a real person, conduct to avoid.

In summary, 2 Tim. is a personal paraenetic letter. Its rallying cry is: imitate the personal example of Paul and Timothy; resist the bad example of people like Hymenaeus and Philetus (see 2 Tim 2:17).

How is the Formula "In Christ Jesus"
used in the Pastorals?

The "in Christ Jesus" of 2 Tim 1:1 is the first of nine occurrences of this Pauline formula in the Pastorals (see also 1 Tim 1:14; 3:13; 2 Tim 1:9,13; 2:1,10; 3:12,15). In Paul's genuine epistles the phrase is used much more frequently and with greater variations ("in Christ," "in the Lord," "in the Lord Jesus," etc.). And note that the Pastorals are unique in using this formula eight times with abstract nouns, like "life" in 2 Tim 1:1, and once with a verb (2 Tim 3:12). In the genuine Pauline epistles the formula is generally used with persons, has the connotation of "being in Christ," and is perhaps best explained by the analogy of mystical union. See for example, Rom 6:11: "So you also must consider yourselves dead to sin and alive to God *in Christ Jesus*." Or see Phil 3:9: "and be found in him, not having a righteousness of my own, based on law, but that which is through faith *in Christ*, the righteousness from God that depends on faith."

The data of the Pastorals points to a different emphasis in the use of the formula, but an emphasis which is not totally absent from the genuine epistles. See Rom 3:24; 8:39; 1 Cor 4:17 and Gal 1:22 where Paul uses this formula with abstract nouns. It seems that the author of the Pastorals has developed one branch of Paul's use of the formula "in Christ Jesus." Why did he single out that one usage? It is hard to say. The contexts in which he employs the formula suggest that he used it to spotlight the central significance of Jesus Christ for salvation. The abstract nouns which this formula modifies detail what Christ Jesus has done for the believer, e.g., he has effected *faith*. In 2 Tim 1:1 "in Christ Jesus" modifies "promise of life"; fullness of life will be the consequence of what Christ Jesus has effected in the person of the believer.

As we travel through the Pastorals, we will have other occasions to note how their author has maintained ties with Pauline tradition. To his generation he does not hand on ten volumes of the collected works of Paul, but gives a précis of

Paul's essential teachings. His use of the Pauline formula, "in Christ Jesus," is one such précis.

CHRISTIAN FAITH HAS DEEP ROOTS.
2 Tim 1:3-5.

> ³I thank God whom I serve with a clear conscience, as did my fathers, when I remember you constantly in my prayers. ⁴As I remember your tears, I long night and day to see you, that I may be filled with joy. ⁵I am reminded of your sincere faith, a faith that dwelt first in your grandmother Lois and your mother Eunice and now, I am sure, dwells in you.

In the Pauline letter format a thanksgiving prayer normally follows the preface. The author of the Pastorals builds this thanksgiving on the Pauline model, particularly as found in Rom 1:8-12. Here are the significant parallels from the thanksgiving of Romans, a letter, it should be remembered, Paul wrote to a church he did not know firsthand: "I thank my God . . . for all of you . . . whom I serve with my spirit . . . that without ceasing I mention you always in my prayers, asking . . . to come to you. For I long to see you . . . that we may be mutually encouraged by each other's faith, both yours and mine" (Rom 1:8-12). As we move through the Pastorals, I will draw your attention to additional parallels between the Pastorals and other Pauline epistles. These epistles served as one of the bases for the Pauline tradition incorporated in the Pastorals.

The images of Paul in verse three and of Timothy in verse five point to the deep roots which Christian faith enjoys. Paul's faith has sure foundations in God's revelation expressed in the Old Testament. Timothy's is firmly anchored in his Christian family line. By remembering Paul and Timothy in this way, the author has two goals. First, he wants to assure his readers that Christian faith is not a here-today-gone-tomorrow phenomenon. It has authoritative roots in the long history of God's Old Testament revelation, in Christian family traditions, in Paul, and in Timothy. Secondly, he strives to bolster the faith of his church, which like Timothy, needs strengthening to remain loyal to the faith in the face of suffering. This second goal will dominate the next section (1:6-14), which begins with "hence" and draws a vital lesson from the image of Timothy whose "sincere faith" is firmly rooted.

THE SUFFERING PAUL AND THE HANDING ON OF THE DEPOSIT OF FAITH.
2 Tim 1:6-14.

> [6]Hence I remind you to rekindle the gift of God that is within you through the laying on of my hands; [7]for God did not give us a spirit of timidity but a spirit of power and love and self-control.
>
> [8]Do not be ashamed then of testifying to our Lord, nor of me his prisoner, but take your share of suffering for the gospel in the power of God, [9]who saved us and called us with a holy calling, not in virtue of our works but in virtue of his own purpose and the grace which he gave us in Christ Jesus ages ago, [10]and now has manifested through the appearing of our Savior Christ Jesus, who abolished death and brought life and immortality to light through the gospel. [11]For this gospel I was appointed a preacher and apostle and teacher, [12]and therefore I suffer as I do. But I am not ashamed, for I know whom I have believed, and I am sure that he is able to guard until that Day what has been entrusted to me. [13]Follow the pattern of the sound words which you have heard from me, in the faith and love which are in Christ Jesus; [14]guard the truth that has been entrusted to you by the Holy Spirit who dwells within us.

This passage is like a hilltop from which you can see the brilliance of autumn for miles around. We savor the beauty of the Pastorals by looking at this section from four vantage points.

Exhortation to Timothy and His Churches

2 Tim 1:6-14 builds upon the thanksgiving prayer of 1:3-5 (see the connective adverb "hence" at the beginning of verse 6). Because of his deep-rooted faith (1:5) Timothy should be encouraged to preach the gospel fearlessly. Because of the gift he has received through the laying on of hands (1:6) he should move forward into the world preaching the gospel with "power and love and self-control" (1:7). In his preaching, Timothy should draw encouragement and strength from the example of the suffering Paul (1:12-13). Timothy's preaching of the gospel sets up a meeting with the person of Christ Jesus, Savior. And as Timothy should know from having met that same Jesus, Jesus supports and sets his preachers' hearts on fire. It is understandable that Timothy would be apprehensive in the face of his awesome charge of preaching the gospel in difficult times. But by reflecting on the gift God has bestowed on him, by cherishing the example of the apostle Paul, and by deepening his love for Jesus whose gospel he preaches, Timothy will guard "the truth that has been entrusted to him by the Holy Spirit who dwells within us" (1:14).

Guarding What Has Been Entrusted -
Safeguarding The Deposit of Faith

Let us explore three key verses. In each one a single Greek word, which literally means "deposit," is translated by "what has been entrusted":

> And I am sure that he is able to guard until that Day what has been entrusted to me (2 Tim 1:12).

> Guard the truth that has been entrusted to you by the Holy Spirit who dwells within us (2 Tim 1:14).

> O Timothy, guard what has been entrusted to you (1 Tim 6:20; see also 2 Tim 1:13; 2:2 where similar ideas are expressed).

From 2 Tim 1:12,14 one can get the impression, an impression reinforced by many commentators, that the "deposit of faith" is something static. According to this impression, Timothy is being exhorted to preserve intact a package of truths, creeds, and regulations he has received from Paul. He is to hand that package on to trustworthy people, who in turn will preserve it intact and pass it on to other trustworthy people in the next generation. I suggest to you that this impression needs correction, for it views "deposit" or "what has been entrusted" literalistically and not figuratively. Here is my point. It is true that the word "deposit" is a legal term and indicates that what had been entrusted to a person's keeping should be kept unused and undamaged until the party claims it back. But that legal term can also be used figuratively as Philo of Alexandria, a Jewish philosopher and contemporary of Paul, did in his *Who Is The Heir of Divine Things?*, paragraphs 103-111 where he discussed preserving God's trust of soul, speech, and sense.

If we view "deposit" literalistically, we run the risk of seeing it as some physical object, like a family heirloom which you leave with a neighbor for safekeeping while you go on vacation. Your neighbor is faithful and trustworthy when she or he hands your heirloom back to you intact. But how does one hand on or guard something "spiritual" like Paul's teaching on justification by faith and not by works of the Law? How does one preserve the spirit a foundress of a religious congregation has entrusted to her Sisters, e.g., the apostolate of educating the poor? How does one safeguard the Constitution of one's country in circumstances which the founding mothers and fathers never foresaw?

Yes, the "deposit" of faith should be seen figuratively. What analogies will help us interpret the preservation of a "deposit" which is spiritual? I suggest two related analogies. Since Paul is presented as the example/pattern for Timothy to follow, I suggest the analogies of friendship and of handing on the family name. First, the analogy of friendship, of preserving the confidences entrusted to us by a friend. The sharing of friends makes us grow, so much so that we become better persons because of the sharing. The friend's love and example enable, inspire, and co-create us. What we hand on to others in our lives is the goodness that our friend has accomplished in us. Let's take this analogy of friendship deeper and move into the realm of our friendship with Jesus Christ. (Recall what the author says about Paul's personal relationship with Jesus Christ, "For I know whom I have believed," in verse 12.) When we have benefited from the sharing of our friend Jesus, we must tell others about his goodness. Just as a friend may sing the praises of his or her best friend, so too the one who has been entrusted with the truth of the gospel—which is Jesus Christ himself—must proclaim its wonders to others. And this sharing of what has been entrusted is not the handing on of a neat package of information or even creeds, but is the witness of a life, is the sharing of memories, life, love, hope and vision.

My second analogy underscores a further aspect of Paul as Timothy's model. In guarding the deposit of the faith, Timothy will be transformed by what his father, Paul, has entrusted to him, his son, as his last will and testament. Timothy will preserve the family name and reputation by embodying in new circumstances his father's vision and virtues. And such embodiment will not be wooden, but dynamic lest the family name fall into disrepute for resting on its laurels.

Lest you think that I am reading my own thoughts into 2 Tim 1:12,14, I invite you to tour the way the author of the Pastorals guards the Pauline deposit of faith in this very passage.

An Example of How the Author Guards the Pauline Deposit of Faith

For our example I focus on a major aspect of the Pauline deposit of faith: justification by faith and not by works of the Law (see also the commentary on Titus 3:1-11). A careful reading of 2 Tim 1:9 will show that the author's intention is to bring the kernel of Paul's teaching into a new age where people are not fighting over *works of the Law* anymore. A comparison of 2 Tim 1:9 with pertinent Pauline passages will highlight the Pauline deposit of faith; I italicize the main points:

2 Tim 1:9 - Who *saved* us and *called us with a holy calling, not in virtue of our works* but in virtue of his own *purpose* and the *grace* which he gave us in Christ Jesus ages ago.

Rom 3:28 - For we hold that a man is justified by faith *apart from works of law.*

Eph 2:8-9 - For *by grace* you have been *saved* through faith; and this is not your own doing, it is the gift of God - *not because of works*, lest any man should boast.

Like the author of Eph 2:8-9 the author of the Pastorals omits discussion of *works of the Law*. That question, reflected in Rom 3:28, is in the past. But our author is true to the Pauline gospel by retaining Paul's faith insight that humans do not save themselves. God's graciousness in Christ Jesus effects salvation. Expressed negatively, we do not save ourselves "in virtue of our works."

In 2 Tim 1:9 the author of the Pastorals gives evidence of his fidelity to the Pauline deposit of faith. He did not rest on the laurels of his father Paul, but adapted the Pauline heritage to his situation. And if we look at 2 Tim 1:10, we can see further indications of his adaptation. When the followers of Paul took his gospel into the hellenistic world, they had to "update" it in order to communicate with people who spoke a different religious language. In a world which knew of many saviors, Jesus is portrayed as *the* Savior. Jesus brings what hellenistic folk sought from their saviors: life, immortality, abolition of death. However, these gifts of salvation are now defined by the reality of Jesus Christ. But the author knows that a mere reference to the reality of Jesus Christ may not be concrete enough to prevent people from interpreting Jesus' gifts of salvation in a way which bypasses the flesh-and-blood dimensions of life. That is why he interprets the creed-like materials of verses 9-10 by the example of the Paul *who suffers* for the gospel (see verses 11-12). The author reminds Timothy and his churches that steadfastness to the gospel means suffering. But with this observation we are at the threshold of our final point. To it we now turn.

The Situation of the Pastorals - Suffering for the Gospel

2 Tim 1:6-14 confronts us head-on with the reality of suffering for the gospel. Paul is suffering because of his fidelity to Jesus Christ, and exhorts Timothy to perseverance in the face of suffering. But why does the author remember Paul in this light? He surely could have recalled some preaching triumph that Paul had when people flocked to him. Such an image would also have encouraged Timothy. Through the examples of Paul and Timothy the author is encouraging his communities who suffer for the sake of the gospel. If we picture the churches of the Pastorals as suffering in their attempts to bring the gospel to all peoples, we will be frequently enraptured by the stark beauty of the Pastorals.

EXAMPLES OF NOT BEING ASHAMED OF THE GOSPEL.
2 Tim 1:15-18.

> [15]You are aware that all who are in Asia turned away from me, and among them Phygelus and Hermogenes. [16]May the Lord grant mercy to the household of Onesiphorus, for he often refreshed me; he was not ashamed of my chains, [17]but when he arrived in Rome he searched for me eagerly and found me—[18]may the Lord grant him to find mercy from the Lord on that Day—and you well know all the service he rendered at Ephesus.

The motto of 2 Tim is captured in the old Latin proverb, "Verba docent, exampla trahunt"—"Words teach, examples captivate." This section rings out this motto loud and clear.

In the General Introduction to the Pastorals, I discussed their pseudonymous character, that is, that a follower of Paul wrote them in Paul's name with the intention of proclaiming Paul's gospel to a new generation. This passage, chuck full of personal reminiscences, does not go counter to that proposal. It was no secret that Paul's missionary activity, especially in Asia, was not a bed of roses. Recall 2 Cor 1:8: "For we do not want you to be ignorant, brethren, of the affliction we experienced in Asia; for we were so utterly, unbearably crushed that we despaired of life itself." In his customary way, the author of the Pastorals has expanded this information (see the "all" of verse 15) and made it concrete by the addition of the personal names of Phygelus, Hermogenes, and Onesiphorus. His purpose in doing this was not to provide biographical data, but to make an important theological point via personal examples. A closer examination of "ashamed" (verse 16) will acquaint us with the point.

In the Pastorals "ashamed" occurs three times. And all three occurrences are found in chapter one of 2 Tim:

> Do not be *ashamed* then of testifying to the Lord, nor of me his prisoner, but take your share of suffering for the gospel (verse 8).

> And therefore I suffer as I do. But I am not *ashamed*, for I know whom I have believed (verse 12).

> He (Onesiphorus) was not *ashamed* of my chains (verse 16).

> (See also Mk 8:38: "For whoever is *ashamed* of me and of my words in this adulterous and sinful generation, of him will the Son of man also be *ashamed.*")

The verb "ashamed" shows how 2 Tim 1:15-18 is intimately connected in thought with the preceding section. Whereas other friends like Phygelus and Hermogenes were ashamed of and abandoned Paul, Onesiphorus was faithful to him. Timothy should follow the example of Paul and Onesiphorus and not be ashamed of suffering for Jesus.

We contemporary followers of Jesus draw encouragement from Paul's example. We will not allow fear of rejection to stand in the way of our preaching the gospel in word and in deed.

GOD'S FIDELITY ENABLES ENDURANCE IN SUFFERING.
2 Tim 2:1-13.

2 You then, my son, be strong in the grace that is in Christ Jesus, ²and what you have heard from me before many witnesses entrust to faithful men who will be able to teach others also. ³Take your share of suffering as a good soldier of Christ Jesus. ⁴No soldier on service gets entangled in civilian pursuits, since his aim is to satisfy the one who enlisted him. ⁵An athlete is not crowned unless he competes according to the rules. ⁶It is the hard-working farmer who ought to have the first share of the crops. ⁷Think over what I say, for the Lord will grant you understanding in everything.

⁸Remember Jesus Christ, risen from the dead, descended from David, as preached in my gospel, ⁹the gospel for which I am suffering and wearing fetters like a criminal. But the word of God is not fettered. ¹⁰Therefore I endure everything for the sake of the elect, that they also may obtain the salvation which in Christ Jesus goes with eternal glory. ¹¹The saying is sure:

If we have died with him, we shall also live with him;
¹²If we endure, we shall also reign with him;
if we deny him, he also will deny us;
¹³if we are faithless, he remains faithful—
for he cannot deny himself.

Recently I participated in a discussion with a noted biblical scholar. It was a delight to see him creatively working through answers to difficult questions. In this section we will learn much by seeing how the author of the Pastorals creatively works through answers to the difficult question of how to endure suffering for the gospel's sake.

Endurance During Suffering for the Gospel

In these verses the author continues his exhortation to Timothy that he endure suffering in preaching the gospel. As in previous sections the example of Paul is a chief inspiration for that exhortation. See especially verses 8-10. Paul's gospel proclaims that the suffering and death of Jesus did not veto God's promises made to David. God raised Jesus from the dead. And Paul preaches this gospel not only in word, but also by his life. If he would flee from suffering and martyrdom, he would be placing his loyalties elsewhere and in effect saying that God is not to be trusted. Just as life came from the suffering and death of Jesus, so too does life come from Paul's suffering as the word of God goes forth and as the elect are given salvation (verses 9-10). But life issues forth through suffering only because Paul "endures" (see verses 10, 12). For Timothy, for church leaders like him, and for countless others Paul is *the* example of endurance in the faithful preaching of the gospel.

But the author of the Pastorals is not content to exhort Timothy via the personal example of Paul as if a mere external model would be sufficient to carry Timothy through dire situations. The author reminds him of the power of the grace given him by Christ Jesus (verse 1). His conduct should flow from the faith he has, a faith which "remembers" that in Jesus Christ God has shown himself as a God who gives life to the dead (verse 8). He is also reminded by the "sure saying" of verses 11-13 that his union with Christ empowers him to endure and that Jesus Christ is faithful to his promise of standing by those united to him.

In this secton it is very easy to get the impression that the author's exhortations center on Timothy and church leaders and do not apply to "ordinary" Christians. But that impression would not be accurate. Here is an analogy. Suppose you hear a sermon about the great doctor and bishop St. Augustine of Hippo. If you are not a bishop or learned person, you might easily think that you cannot draw any inspiration from his life. That is, until the preacher tells about Augustine's struggle to see God's will in his life. Then the lights might flash in your mind. Here is a part of Augustine's life which has great meaning for you. I suggest that something similar is happening behind the scenes of verses 3-7. There is nothing in these verses which restricts their meaning to Timothy as a church leader. Or put another way, these verses are the author's way of universalizing his message from the examples of Paul and Timothy. "Take your share of suffering as a good soldier of Christ Jesus" (verse 3) is an exhortation for all Christians. The examples of soldier, athlete, and farmer in verses 4-6 are open-ended, that is, they have no single meaning. For example, on one level the examples of soldier, athlete, and farmer show that from hardship comes success. On another level, the soldier teaches the lesson of singlemindedness, the athlete the lesson of self-denial, the farmer the lesson of intense effort. Thus, there is no pat way in which "dying with" (verse 11) and "enduring" (verse 12) are to be carried out. "Think over what I say" (verse 7) is very important advice. Like the preacher whose theme is the virtues of St. Augustine, the author of the Pastorals goes beyond those virtues which may be the unique preserve of the bishop and doctor and provides a message for all. For all will suffer for the gospel, be it by ridicule, blacklisting, physical abuse or whatever.

The Saying Is Sure

The hymnic material of verses 11-13 is introduced by the formula "the saying is sure." This formula occurs four other times in the Pastorals: 1 Tim 1:15; 3:1; 4:8 and Titus 3:4-7. In 1 Tim 1:15 and 4:8 the formula is expanded: "The saying is sure and worthy of full acceptance." From these two passages we can infer that the formula is not only one which marks off a quotation, but also one which indicates that the content of the quotation is trustworthy. The sure sayings will guide the reader in faith (see 1 Tim 1:15; 2 Tim 2:11-13; Titus 3:4-7) and in practice (see 1 Tim 3:1; 4:8). The "sure sayings" are those which the communities of the Pastorals have come to cherish as reliable guides to faith and life. They help members of the communities answer important and new questions.

In thinking through the functions of these "sure sayings" in the Pastorals, I have found the following analogies helpful. You may, too. How often in my priestly life I have been guided by the scholastic saying about the sacraments: the sacraments are for people (sacramenta propter hominem). In a hospital where the patient had multiple tubes and complex apparatus on all sides I bypassed rubrics and administered the sacrament of anointing in the most human way possible. People evaluate a situation of immense suffering or of great religious success with the saying: There is no crown without the cross. In this connection I recall a saying of my novice master: the crib, the cross, the ciborium. Through this alliterative saying he was communicating the nature and presence of God in Jesus Christ. There is a wealth of faith experience and communal discernment of Spirit behind the "sure sayings." They are rhythmic, pithy, and easily remembered. They can be applied to a host of situations. In a final section we take a closer look at one of these sure sayings, that of 2 Tim 2:11-13.

2 Tim 2:11-13 - By Itself and In Its Application

The sure saying of 2 Tim 2:11-13 seems to be composed of two statements from Pauline tradition, a statement from the gospel tradition, and a considerable amount of Christian experience. It was probably composed originally for a baptismal celebration. The statements from the Pauline and gospel traditions are:

> "But if we have died with Christ, we believe that we shall also live with him" (Rom 6:8).

"And if children, then heirs, heirs of God and fellow heirs with Christ, provided we suffer with him in order that we may also be glorified with him" (Rom 8:17).

"But whoever denies me before men, I also will deny before my Father who is in heaven" (Mt 10:33).

God's fidelity enables Christians to sustain the union with Christ they began at baptism.

The author of the Pastorals applies the sure saying of verses 11-13 to help Christians make sense out of persecution. Paul is the example of one who "endured" (see verses 10,12), and now reigns with Jesus Christ. And the secret of Paul's endurance was God's faithfulness. By the example of Paul the author exhorts Timothy and other Christians to steadfastness in suffering for the gospel's sake. He exhorts them to recall the faith they profess. But most importantly he exhorts them to deepen their faith in Jesus Christ with whom they are united.

THE LORD UPHOLDS HIS CHURCH WHICH EXPERIENCES HERESY.
2 Tim 2:14-26

[14]Remind them of this, and charge them before the Lord to avoid disputing about words, which does no good, but only ruins the hearers. [15]Do your best to present yourself to God as one approved, a workman who has no need to be ashamed, rightly handling the word of truth. [16]Avoid such godless chatter, for it will lead people into more and more ungodliness, [17]and their talk will eat its way like gangrene. Among them are Hymenaeus and Philetus, [18]who have swerved from the truth by holding that the resurrection is past already. They are upsetting the faith of some. [19]But God's firm foundation stands, bearing this seal: "The Lord knows those who are his," and, "Let every one who names the name of the Lord depart from iniquity."

²⁰In a great house there are not only vessels of gold and silver but also of wood and earthenware, and some for noble use, some for ignoble. ²¹If any one purifies himself from what is ignoble, then he will be a vessel for noble use, consecrated and useful to the master of the house, ready for any good work. ²²So shun youthful passions and aim at righteousness, faith, love, and peace, along with those who call upon the Lord from a pure heart. ²³Have nothing to do with stupid, senseless controversies; you know that they breed quarrels. ²⁴And the Lord's servant must not be quarrelsome but kindly to every one, an apt teacher, forbearing, ²⁵correcting his opponents with gentleness. God may perhaps grant that they will repent and come to know the truth, ²⁶and they may escape from the snare of the devil, after being captured by him to do his will.

While in San Francisco some time back, I toured St. Mary's Cathedral, whose outward design has been unfairly compared with the agitator of a washing machine. It took much exploration, much contemplation, and much patience before the cathedral's majestic beauty captivated me. But now it has a special place in my artist's heart. We come to an important passage in 2 Tim, but a passage which will not yield its beauty easily. We look at it from a number of angles, patiently trying to capture its wisdom.

The Author's Message

Stripped of all embellishment, this section conveys these lessons. First, for church leaders. They are to remind the people of God of the meaning of Paul's gospel and example ("Remind them of this" in verse 14 refers back to verses 8-13). Preaching of this sort will edify people whereas splitting of hairs will just show how irrelevant religion is to daily life (verse 14). Church leaders were earlier admonished not to be ashamed of suffering persecution for the gospel's sake (see 2 Tim 1:8,12,16). Here they are admonished not to be ashamed of preaching a gospel which will meet with the opposition of heresy (verse 15). The admonition that church leaders shun "youthful passions" (verse 22) is not a reference to sex, but to the passions of intolerance, arrogance, quick temper and the like. Church leaders should deal kindly with opponents and realize that faith and repentance are gifts of God and not won by skillful argumentation or power plays which grind an opponent into the dust (verses 25-26).

Second, lessons for "ordinary" Christians. Heresy is part of the air the church breathes, but people should be encouraged that God will not allow his firm foundation to crumble (verse 19). The church's surest weapon against heresy is the pursuit of virtue and holiness (verses 19-21).

Perhaps, the author presents a message which is not very comforting. He does not advise the church to erect a fortress impregnable to all opponents, but to take the risk of going out into the streets of the world with the gospel. While others claim that their teaching flows beautifully from the gospel, you must hold fast to your version of the gospel and prove, by your good works, that it is the "truth."

How The Author Thinks

The author of the Pastorals thinks quite differently from most of us. This is largely due to his use of the literary form of an exhortatory letter (see the section entitled "What Kind of Letter is 2 Timothy?" in the commentary on 2 Tim 1:1-2). The author thinks by means of contrasts, e.g., the false teacher is greedy; the good teacher is the opposite. See the contrasts between 2:14 and 2:15; 2:16 and 2:22; 2:23 and 2:24. In the latter case the words "quarrels".of verse 23 is picked up in verse 24 by "must not be quarrelsome." The author also argues by association of ideas. The sequence of verses 16-22 is a good example of such reasoning.

In verse 16 the author inveighs against godless chatter which will lead people to more and more ungodliness. In verses 17 and 18 he gives an example of such godless chatter and its results. In verse 19 he says that such godless chatter will not destroy God's firm foundation, and alludes to a similar situation in Israel's history when Korah challenged the leadership of Moses (see Numbers 16 and the next paragraph). The phrase "firm foundation" leads the author to the image of "great house" (verses 20-21). "Great house" leads him to the image of the house's "vessels," some of which are for noble use and some for ignoble use. Mention of "ignoble" leads him to talk about purification from what is ignoble. In verse 22 he catalogues the virtues which should be present in those who call upon the Lord with a purified heart. Thus the author has come full circle: he began with the admonition to avoid godless chatter which leads to ungodliness (verse 16), gave examples of that ungodliness (verses 17-18), advised his readers to "depart from iniquity" (verse 19), to purify themselves (verse 21), and to have a pure heart (verse 22).

We can appreciate the author's thought even more clearly if we ferret out the Exodus story of Numbers 16 which seems to lie behind the ideas of verse 19. In this story Korah and two others challenge the leadership of Moses and Aaron. When Moses hears of their objections, he says: "In the morning *the Lord will show who is his*, and who is holy, and will cause him to come near to him; him whom he will choose he will cause to come near to him" (Num 16:5). As the story progresses, Moses tells the congregation: "*Depart, I pray you, from the tents of these wicked men*, and touch nothing of theirs, lest you be swept away with all their sins" (Num 16:26). I have italicized the words which parallel the two sayings found on the plaque of God's firm foundation. The parallels of the Exodus story of 2 Tim 2:19 end here, for, in the churches of the Pastorals, the Lord does not make a visible judgment between the true leaders and the heretics as he did in the Israelite congregation (see Num 16:31-32 where the earth swallows up Korah and companions).

For the author of the Pastorals the church is composed of both saints and sinners, a mixture of vessels for noble use and of vessels for ignoble use. Rather than bemoan that fact, the Pauline Christian "departs from iniquity" and aims at "righteousness, faith, love, and peace."

Disputing With Words; Senseless Controversies

The passages in which the author scores "senseless controversies" and the like include 1 Tim 1:4-7; 4:6-7; 6:3-5,20-21; 2 Tim 2:14,16-18,23-25; Titus 3:8-9. As we have seen from our commentaries on 2 Tim 1:6-14 and 2:1-13 the author is not against theological argumentation as such. But what he rails against are speculations which do not lead to an improvement of Christian life. It would be like us disputing over issues like the following: How many angels can dance on the head of a pin? If God is all-powerful, could he make a square-circle? Will a gold, silver, or brass trumpet usher in the final judgment? Disputing over these issues would not promote Christian virtue.

In denouncing vain speculation, the author of the Pastorals builds upon a contemporary theme and contrasts the teaching of Timothy with that of vain philosophers and sophists. In a passage from Athenagoras' *A Plea for The Christians*, there is a full-blown example of the theme our author hints at:

> For who of those that reduce syllogisms, and clear up ambiguities, and explain etymologies, or of those who teach homonyms and synonyms, and predicaments and axioms, and what is the subject and the predicate, and who promise their disciples by these and such like instructions to make them happy; who of them have so purged their souls as, instead of hating their enemies, to love them; and, instead of speaking ill of those who have reviled them, to bless them; and to pray for those who plot against their lives? . . . But among us you will find uneducated persons, and artisans, and old women, who, if they are unable in words to prove the benefit of our doctrine, yet by their deeds exhibit the benefit arising from their persuasion of its truth; they do not rehearse speeches, but exhibit good works (paragraph 11 in the translation of *The Ante-Nicene Fathers*).

Christians should not be viewed as philosophers who engage in a useless debate about words. Christians benefit

society and show by their exemplary lives that they worship
God.

2 Tim 2:18 and The Nature of The Heresy
Combatted in The Pastorals

2 Tim 2:18 is one of many passages in which the author
combats heretics. See also 1 Tim 1:3-11; 4:1-7; 6:3-5,20-21;
2 Tim 2:14-4:5; Titus 1:10-16; 3:8-9. Despite the frequency
of this polemic against heretics it is not easy to delineate
the contours of this heresy. There are a number of reasons
for this. First, much of the polemic is stereotyped (see the
commentary on 2 Tim 3:1-9 for more detail on this point.)
Second, the author is engaged in exhortation, not in refutation. For instance, 2 Tim 2:18 occurs in an exhortatory
pattern of contrast between the good teacher and the false
teacher. Within such a literary form there is not much room
for refutation of the false teaching itself. Third, as we have
noted in the General Introduction to this commentary, the
Pastorals are pseudonymous writings. And this means that
their author blends the perspective of Paul's time with his
own. With these cautions in mind, let us focus our attention
on 2 Tim 2:18. The commentaries on the other polemical
passages will provide additional insights, especially on the
"Jewishness" of the heresy.

"The resurrection is past already" (2 Tim 2:18). Paul
himself had difficulty conveying the Christian message of
resurrection of the body to Greeks who tended to have a
negative view of the body (see esp. 1 Cor 15). In Rom 6:1-11,
a passage dealing with the Christian's union with Christ,
Paul had to stress the futurity of the resurrection: "For if we
have been united with him in a death like his, we *shall* cer-
tainly be united with him in a resurrection like his" (Rom
6:5). Resurrection is future and for the total human person,
body and soul. But Hymenaeus (see 1 Tim 1:20), Philetus,
and others teach that the resurrection is past already. That
is, they are teaching that by their knowledge (*gnosis* in
Greek) of Jesus Christ as Savior their real self or spiritual
element has already been resurrected. They repudiate bodily

and worldly existence. If this reconstruction of the meaning of the ever-so-brief 2 Tim 2:18 is on target, we can begin to fathom the heretical teaching denounced in 1 Tim 4:1-5. From the opponents' gnostic and world-hating perspective they forbid marriage (and the immersion in matter which sex and procreation imply) and enjoin abstinence from foods (1 Tim 4:3). If the heretics contend that salvation is gained by knowledge, then we can appreciate the Pastorals' stress on knowledge of the truth (see e.g., 2 Tim 2:25 and 1 Tim 6:20). Put succinctly, the opponents are guilty of far more than failure to repeat an article of the creed like "I believe in the resurrection of the body." Their position undermines the goodness of God's creation, the value of the body, involvement in history, social justice, to say nothing of evacuating Christian hope of all meaning.

The gnostic heresy is indeed pernicious. The author advises that it and other heresies are a part of the church's daily life. Such heresies can be combatted best by virtuous church leaders who continue to develop the Pauline deposit of faith and by Christians who show the world that their faith is not gangrenous, but healthy, that is, productive of morally upright conduct.

We have explored the wisdom of 2 Tim 2:14-26 from four different angles. In the commentary of 1 Tim 3:14-16 I will have further opportunity to share insights on what the author means by church. In this section he has teased us with his views on this important topic.

TAKE COURAGE: THE HERETICS' SUCCESS IS TRANSITORY.
2 Tim 3:1-9.

> **3** But understand this, that in the last days there will come times of stress. ²For men will be lovers of self, lovers of money, proud, arrogant, abusive, disobedient to their parents, ungrateful, unholy, ³inhuman, implacable, slanderers, profligates, fierce, haters of good, ⁴treacherous, reckless, swollen with conceit, lovers of

pleasure rather than lovers of God, [5]holding the form of religion but denying the power of it. Avoid such people. [6]For among them are those who make their way into households and capture weak women, burdened with sins and swayed by various impulses, [7]who will listen to anybody and can never arrive at a knowledge of the truth. [8]As Jannes and Jambres opposed Moses, so these men also oppose the truth, men of corrupt mind and counterfeit faith; [9]but they will not get very far, for their folly will be plain to all, as was that of those two men.

This passage has so many stereotyped elements that it is difficult to read its meaning straightaway. I count four stock themes: 1) during the last days sinners will abound (verses 1-4); 2) these people do not practice what they preach (verse 5); 3) gullible women (verses 6-7); 4) temporary success is followed by ignominy (verses 8-9).

Lest you think that these stock items are foreign to our way of thinking, let me share some contemporary examples. For verses 1-4: "With all these weird kooks running around, forcing people to commit suicide and what-have-you, it must be the end of the world." For verse 5: "Those priests preach eloquently about patience and then turn around and loudly rebuke the altar boys for not holding the cruets right. They wrench the heart out of their sermons." For verses 6-7: "There go the bored suburban housewives stampeding to pay $50 for a two-hour workshop on "How To Cope." They'll work at putting into practice what they learned until the next "self-help" expert parades into town. Then they'll join that parade. How can they learn anything when they flit from fad to fad!" For verses 8-9: "Remember how the Watergate people stonewalled the pursuit of justice. It seemed like moral integrity in government was a pipe-dream. But their moment of power has come and gone. Why, it's hard even to remember their names."

Now that these examples have put us on the wavelength of the author of the Pastorals, let us briefly consider some ancient parallels to the stereotyped materials he uses in this section. Relative to verse 1, Jewish and Christian thinkers maintained that in the last days evil would multiply. Recall the words of Jesus: "And then many will fall away, and betray one another, and hate one another. And many false prophets will arise and lead many astray. And because wickedness is multiplied, most men's love will grow cold" (Mt 24:10-12). It is important to note that whereas verses 1-2 use the future tense "will," the admonition, "Avoid such people," in verse 5 indicates that the author believes that these sinners are present in his own churches.

Verses 2-5 contain a "catalogue of vices." A similar catalogue is found in Rom 1:29-32. The purpose of the catalogue is not to detail the vices of any one person. It shows the readers that the conduct of the heretics is light years away from the religion they profess (verse 5). A comparable use of a catalogue of vices is found in Philo of Alexandria, a Jewish philosopher and contemporary of Paul:

> And nevertheless they (the sophists) entertain all the time sentiments quite at variance with the things which they say. At the very moment when they are singing the praises of good sense and moderation and righteousness and piety, they are found to be more than ever practising foolishness, licentiousness, injustice, and impiety, and to be confounding and overturning, you may well nigh say, every ordinance of God or man (Loeb translation of *The Worse Attacks the Better,* 73).

Two things make verses 6-7 difficult to interpret. First, pagan, Jewish, and Christian polemical authors frequently charge that their opponents taught women with the sole purpose of seducing them. Is our author employing this stereotyped charge to malign his opponents? It does not seem so since he does not explicitly denounce them for unchaste conduct. Secondly, the culture of the times almost totally denied women advanced education and placed rich women in a position where they had time on their hands. These women sought out the latest in religion. There is a telling parallel in the account St. Irenaeus gives of the Valentinian gnostic Marcus (*Adversus Haereses* 1.13,3):

> He concerns himself in particular with women, especially those of high rank, the elegantly attired and wealthy, whom he frequently attempts to lead astray by flattering them and saying, 'I desire to make thee a partaker of my Grace, since the Father of all doth continuously behold thy angel before his face' (translation from W. Foerster, *Gnosis* I, p. 201).

From the evidence of verses 6-7 it seems that the heretics were like travelling philosophers and that they did have success among women. For more detail on the role of women in the Pastorals, see the commentary on 1 Tim 2:8-15.

Behind verses 8-9 is the Exodus story of the ten plagues. The key verses of the story are these: "So Moses and Aaron went to Pharaoh and did as the Lord commanded; Aaron cast down his rod before Pharaoh and his servants, and it became a serpent. Then Pharaoh summoned the wise men and the sorcerers; and they also, the magicians of Egypt, did the same by their secret arts" (7:10-11). After some time the magicians are vanquished. Later Jewish tradition gave the names of Jannes and Jambres to these wise men and magicians. The reason the author alludes to Jannes and Jambres in verses 8-9 is not because they were magicians, but because their success against Moses was short-lived. The Exodus accounts of what God did for Moses against Korah (see 2 Tim 2:19) and against Jannes and Jambres give the author the means of forecasting what God will do for the leaders in the churches of Paul.

Through these stereotyped elements about the heretics the author connects this section with 2:14-26 and gives some powerful admonitions to Timothy, those in his churches, and to us. First, there will be people in your congregation who will profess the same religion that you do, but their conduct will show that they have not made their faith part of their daily lives. Second, wandering teachers will have success among those who fill their calendars with the latest religious fads. Do not chase after fads, but hand on the deposit of faith in such a way that it speaks to contemporary needs. Finally, as the history of Israel and of the church teaches, the future is bright for those who persevere in faithfully adapting God's word in tumultuous times.

THE LORD EQUIPS HIS PEOPLE DURING TRIALS. 2 Tim 3:10-17.

[10]Now you have observed my teaching, my conduct, my aim in life, my faith, my patience, my love, my steadfastness, [11]my persecutions, my sufferings, what befell me at Antioch, at Iconium, and at Lystra, what persecutions I endured; yet from them all the Lord rescued me. [12]Indeed all who desire to live a godly life in Christ Jesus will be persecuted, [13]while evil men and impostors will go on from bad to worse, deceivers and deceived. [14]But as for you, continue in what you have learned and have firmly believed, knowing from whom you learned it [15]and how from childhood you have been acquainted with the sacred writings which are able to instruct you for salvation through faith in Christ Jesus. [16]All scripture is inspired by God and profitable for teaching, for reproof, for correction, and for training in righteousness, [17]that the man of God may be complete, equipped for every good work.

When I first started playing golf, a friend gave me three rules: "First, keep your eye on the ball. Second, keep your eye on the ball. Third, keep your eye on the ball!" When I followed that advice, I shot a good round of golf. When I didn't, I threw my coordination off and sometimes missed the ball completely! In commenting on this epistle, I have had to remind myself time and again of the three basic rules for intepreting the Pastorals. "First, they are exhortation. Second, they are exhortatory letters. Third, their purpose is exhortation, not the doing of systematic theology." Keeping these basic rules in front of our minds, let us probe this passage at three points.

First, a few words on how this section relates to the exhortations which preceded it. By putting into practice the Pauline virtues enumerated in verses 10-11, Timothy and others will show that their teaching, unlike that of the heretics denounced in 3:1-9, leads to virtue. Verses 10-12, with their accent on the theme of persecution, relate back to 2 Tim 1:6-2:13 where a similar theme was struck. Verses 13-17 relate well with the theme of combatting heretics which was on stage in 2 Tim 2:14-3:9. In a sense, then, this passage is a summary of the two themes of how to behave when persecution and heresy rage.

Second, exhortation often blends the past, the near past, and the present. (For more detail on this point, see the example of a contemporary paraenetic letter in the commentary on 2 Tim 1:1-2.) In verses 10-11 Paul is the example from the past for Timothy, and Timothy is the example from the near past for the church leaders at the time of the author. In verses 12-17 the author draws lessons from both Paul and Timothy for all Christians in his churches. Let me explain in greater detail what I mean by exploring the meanings of "observed" (verse 10) and "man of God" (verse 17).

When you note the things which Timothy has "observed," you begin to suspect that more is involved in discipleship than observing Paul with a pair of binoculars. The verb "observe" is a technical term of discipleship, and in this context means that Timothy has embodied Paul's virtues and experiences in his own life. Seen from another perspective, Timothy is depicted in verses 10-11 as a model, stalwart, veteran Christian leader whereas in 2 Tim 1:6-2:13 he was painted as an almost cowardly, green recruit in Paul's service. In this passage the author lifts up Timothy as an example for his church leaders and for all Christians. In brief, persecuted Christians can draw encouragement from the examples of Paul and Timothy whom God rescued from harm. "Indeed *all* who desire to live a godly life in Christ Jesus will be persecuted" (verse 12).

"Man of God" (verse 17; the Greek for "man" is a generic word which includes both women and men) can too easily be interpreted as priest or church leader because of our culture and Roman Catholic tradition. But the phrase refers to all Christians. The best illuminative parallel to this meaning is found in the document called *Letter of Aristeas* 140, which refers to all Jews as "men of God": "Hence the leading Egyptian priests having looked carefully into many matters, and being cognizant with our affairs, call us 'men of God.' This is a title which does not belong to the rest of mankind but only to those who worship the true God. The rest are men not of God, but of meats and drinks and clothing" (translation from R. H. Charles, ed., *The Apocrypha and Pseudepigrapha of the Old Testament II*). This parallel shows that a "man of God" is any Christian who serves God. Such a person is the one outfitted by the study of scripture for every good work.

To summarize my second observation, the author uses the virtues of Paul and Timothy to exhort his contemporaries, who should serve God no matter what the cost.

Third and finally, it remains for us to link verses 15-17 with exhortation. While the author maintains the inspired nature of the scriptures, his purpose here is not to expound that point like a systematic theologian. His purpose is exhortation: the scriptures are seen from the perspective of how they contribute to the building up of Christian life. In all honesty, I must note that while the author upholds the exhortatory importance of the scriptures, he infrequently uses them in his exhortations. Commentators like J. L. Houlden go too far, though, when they write: "A *bon mot* with regard to this verse notes that it is the mark of a mediocre mind to revere so highly that which is so little exploited" (*The Pastoral Epistles*, p. 127, note). Like Paul, the author employs other sources to motivate his exhortations: Pauline tradition of what God has done in Christ Jesus (see the commentary of Titus 2:1-15); the irreproachable conduct expected of Christians by their pagan neighbors (see the commentary on 1 Tim 3:1-13). Though he values the sacred writings highly, the author employs them as one source among the many he uses in his exhortatory letters.

At the end of the commentary on this section, the faithful reader may well ask: "What lessons do these exhortations contain for me?" I offer two suggestions. A friend, a very dedicated Christian, expressed one of the meanings of this passage quite well when he questioned: "I see these people driving around in luxury cars, swapping wives, blind to injustices, and I wonder whether I'm not a fool for Christ, but just a plain fool. Have I missed the meaning of life?" The trials associated with trying to live one's faith in a pluralistic society are not confined to Paul and Asia Minor in the first century A.D. These trials are alive and well in our daily lives. "If we endure, we shall also reign with him" (2 Tim 2:12). With each passing day of scripture study and meditation I learn more deeply the meaning of verse 17. Pondering the scriptures challenges me to repent, makes me seek wholeness, prepares me for the tasks God has in store, and impels me to share the treasure of the scriptures with others. God's Word is profitable beyond all imagining.

PAUL, THE MODEL EMBODIMENT OF THE GOSPEL OF CHRIST CRUCIFIED.
2 Tim 4:1-8.

4 I charge you in the presence of God and of Christ Jesus who is to judge the living and the dead, and by his appearing and his kingdom: [2]preach the word, be urgent in season and out of season, convince, rebuke, and exhort, be unfailing in patience and in teaching. [3]For the time is coming when people will not endure sound teaching, but having itching ears they will accumulate for themselves teachers to suit their own likings, [4]and will turn away from listening to the truth and wander into myths. [5]As for you, always be steady, endure suffering, do the work of an evangelist, fulfil your ministry.

⁶For I am already on the point of being sacrificed; the time of my departure has come. ⁷I have fought the good fight, I have finished the race, I have kept the faith. ⁸Henceforth there is laid up for me the crown of righteousness, which the Lord, the righteous judge, will award to me on that Day, and not only to me but also to all who have loved his appearing.

Simple words like "I love you" or "I'm sorry" can have powerful consequences. The connective "for" at the beginning of verse 6 is such a simple word. It sets us on a trail to a powerful encounter with the theology of the author of the Pastorals. In verses 1-5 the author presents heavy exhortations for Timothy and those like him. In beginning verse 6 with "for," the author intends to give the reasons for these awesome exhortations. The reason is not to be found in the fact that Paul is about to be executed and needs to leave Timothy behind to carry on the task of preaching the gospel. In verses 6-8 Paul is being set up as a model, whose example is the motivating force for the exhortations of verses 1-5. Allow me to explicate my point in the following paragraphs.

What we find in verses 6-8 are not words which Paul would have said about himself. Salvation was not such an assured fact for Paul. As he told the Philippians: "Not that I have already obtained this or am already perfect; but I press on to make it my own, because Christ Jesus has made me his own. Brethren, I do not consider that I have made it my own; but one thing I do, forgetting what lies behind and straining forward to what lies ahead, I press on toward the goal for the prize of the upward call of God in Christ Jesus" (Phil 3:12-14). Behind 2 Tim 4:6-8 stands a later author who is assured of Paul's status with God and holds him up as a model. But a model of what?

First, Paul is the model for church leaders, like Timothy, who by their steadfast preaching will be a bulwark against false teaching. Second, in his suffering (see verses 5: "endure suffering" and verse 6: "being sacrificed") he is a model for all Christians, who strive to live out the gospel message of Christ crucified. This message is also found in 1:8, 12; 2:3; 3:10-11, and especially in 2:8-13. The example of a Paul who is about to be executed in prison for the sake of the gospel gives a lived interpretation to the creeds about "life from death" (2 Tim 2:8) and "if we have died with him, we shall also live with him" (2 Tim 2:11). (See the commentaries on 1 Tim 1:12-17 and 1 Tim 2:1-7 where the author also interprets creeds with events from the life of Paul.) Third, Paul is a model of the ideal Christian, the "person of God" (2 Tim 3:17), who has finished the race successfully and kept trust with the Lord.

Lest the points I made in the preceding paragraph appear dense, I will illustrate them with two contemporary examples. First, parents can instruct their children to show hospitality to guests. This family principle can remain "up in the air" for the children until they see their parents illustrate it by their conduct of hanging up the coats of the guests, showing them to a comfortable seat, asking whether they would like refreshments, and the like. Example breathes life into the principle. So too the life of a suffering Paul breathes life into the Pauline principles found in 2 Tim, especially in 2:8-13. Second, I recall the closing liturgy at a weekend retreat. When it was time to recite the creed, the celebrant asked us to share the most important point in our personal creed. A cripple, someone who had obviously suffered much in life, began: "I believe in the goodness of God." That "attribute" of God burned bright with meaning for me, not because of its intrinsic truth, but because of a living example. Throughout 2 Tim the author paints Paul as one who suffers and thus interprets the Pauline legacy of the centrality of Christ crucified.

In the Introduction to 2 Tim I utilized the image of the loss of a loved one as a means of understanding this epistle. In 2 Tim 4:6-8 we encounter another facet of loss: the last words of a dying loved one. The words of verses 6-8 are Paul's last will and testament to his churches and as such are to be cherished, remembered, and reflected upon. They are a beacon for life and an endless source of encouragement. In this connection, I recall a friend describing how his father gave advice, dreamt dreams, and inspired confidence in his family while he lay dying. In verses 6-8 we have Paul's last words - his advice, his vision, his encouragement - for a church which follows in his footsteps during persecution and heresy.

One final note about the image of Paul projected by verses 6-8. Throughout 2 Tim Paul is depicted as loving Christ Jesus so much that his life was an imitation of the Lord's. That Lord had united himself to Paul (see 2 Tim 2:11-13), who, in response, longed to be crowned by that same Lord on the final Day. For the Paul of the Pastorals the second coming of the Lord is not a wellnigh forgotten article of the creed, but the longing of an expectant and loving heart.

THE MARTYR APOSTLE PAUL PREACHES THE GOSPEL AND IS STRENGTHENED BY THE LORD.
2 Tim 4:9-22.

9Do your best to come to me soon. 10For Demas, in love with this present world, has deserted me and gone to Thessalonica; Crescens has gone to Galatia, Titus to Dalmatia. 11Luke alone is with me. Get Mark and bring him with you; for he is very useful in serving me. 12Tychicus I have sent to Ephesus. 13When you come, bring the cloak that I left with Carpus at Troas, also the books, and above all the parchments. 14Alexander the coppersmith did me great harm; the Lord will requite him for his deeds. 15Beware of him yourself, for he strongly opposed our message. 16At my first defense no one took my part; all deserted me. May it not be charged against them! 17But the Lord stood by me and gave me strength to proclaim the word fully, that all the Gentiles might hear it. So I was rescued from the lion's mouth. 18The Lord will rescue me from every evil and save me for his heavenly kingdom. To him be the glory for ever and ever. Amen.

[19]Greet Prisca and Aquila, and the household of Onesiphorus. [20]Erastus remained at Corinth; Trophimus I left ill at Miletus. [21]Do your best to come before winter. Eubulus sends greetings to you, as do Pudens and Linus and Claudia and all the brethren.

[22]The Lord be with your spirit. Grace be with you.

With its long list of names—odd ones at that—you might think that studying this section is as appealing as reading through a telephone directory. But let me share a secret with you: this section is one of the most powerful in all the Pastorals. To appreciate it, however, we must change our way of viewing it. Both you and I have a tendency to view it as providing biographical information about the last days of Paul. Taking refuge in the time-honored educational principle that "repetition is the mother of study," I remind you and myself that 2 Tim is a personal exhortatory letter. That is, 2 Tim gives exhortations to its readers via personal examples, especially those of Paul and Timothy. (For more information on the nature of 2 Tim, see the commentary on 2 Tim 1:1-2.)

If we view 2 Tim 4:9-22 as replete with biographical data about Paul's last days, we are going to involve ourselves in inconsistencies. For example, why does Paul write in verse 11, "Luke alone is with me," and then write in verse 21 about the many Christians who are supporting him: "Eubulus sends greetings to you, as do Pudens and Linus and Claudia and *all* the brethren"? Why does Paul send Tychicus to Ephesus, apparently to set up a mission, when Timothy is already on mission there (see 1 Tim 1:3)? The questions could be multiplied. It seems to me that most of these questions fade into the background when we view this section as part of a personal exhortatory letter which is highlighting the person of Paul as the example for Christian conduct. Let us explore the edifying lessons Paul's life presents in this section.

Let us begin with the troublesome verse 13: "When you come, bring the cloak that I left with Carpus at Troas, also the books, and above all the parchments." It is easy enough to decide that "cloak" means a large, heavy, winter, sleeveless garment and that "parchments" refers to paged notebooks of parchment which contained the sacred writings of the Old Testament. It is less easy to determine the function of this verse in its context. Some commentators, like J. N. D. Kelly, maintain that no one would have invented this verse: "It is extremely unlikely that an imitator in the ancient world would have thought of inventing banal details like these" (*A Commentary on the Pastoral Epistles*, p. 215). But other commentators have scoured the letters found on papyri and discovered that poor people frequently requested friends to bring or send them their winter mantle (we must remember that clothes were handmade at that time and that one did not just pop down to the department store and buy another one when one had left his at home). The details of verse 13 are drawn from this common feature of a letter from a person who is away from home. The author uses these details to give life to two general principles. The example of Paul requesting his mantle illustrates the truth of the teaching found in 1 Tim 6:6-8: "There is great gain in godliness with contentment; for we brought nothing into the world, and we cannot take anything out of the world; but if we have food and clothing, with these we shall be content." Paul is the model poor Christian missionary, who has the bare necessities of life. By requesting the sacred writings in parchment, Paul gives the approval of his life to the teaching of 2 Tim 3:15-17. His preaching stems from his meditation on the sacred writings of the Old Testament.

Paul has experienced desertion and loneliness (verse 16; see verse 11), and is the model of Christian missionaries who are imprisoned. Fellow Christians are ashamed of them and the gospel they preach (see 2 Tim 1:8,12,16). In this situation of giving witness to the gospel, Paul is the ideal martyr, who prays for forgiveness for his persecutors: "May it not be charged against them!" (verse 16; see also Lk

23:34 and Acts 7:60). The ideal martyr Paul is strengthened by the Lord "to proclaim the word fully" and to testify before the Roman authorities (verse 17). Paul testifies to God's plan for salvation as Jesus did: "Jesus, who gave himself as a ransom for all, the testimony to which was borne at the proper time" (1 Tim 2:6); "In the presence of God who gives life to all things, and of Christ Jesus who in his testimony before Pontius Pilate made the good confession" (1 Tim 6:13). Suffering does not muzzle the preacher, but makes his message the more compelling. But all this is possible only because of the Lord's support and care (verses 17-18).

The author has come to the end of his epistle. He has featured Paul as the paradigm and model for his churches. Paul is the fearless apostle and missionary whose life embodies the gospel. Bereft of human support, he is not ashamed to proclaim the gospel that in Christ Jesus there is abolition of death, life, and immortality. In the life of Paul we can see how God acts, how he wills to save us. God calls and strengthens. He entrusts a legacy and keeps it alive. He stands by us and rescues us from evil. The Lord with whom Christians are united is a faithful Lord. Truly, "the Lord will rescue us from every evil and save us for his heavenly kingdom. To him be the glory for ever and ever. Amen."

1 Timothy and Titus

INTRODUCTION TO
1 TIMOTHY AND TITUS

EVEN THE MOST casual of glances reveals that 1 Tim and Titus are very different from 2 Tim. 2 Tim features an imprisoned Paul, about to be executed, whose life of suffering preaches the gospel. The Paul of 1 Tim and Titus, on the other hand, promulgates rules for conduct and church government. How does one explain these differences, especially when you realize that all three epistles were written at the same time by the same author? We can discover an explanation by delving into the author's images of Paul.

An essay by Walter J. Ong, "The Writer's Audience Is Always a Fiction" (*Interfaces of the Word*, pp. 53-81), is most provocative on image-making. Ong observes that authors have to fictionalize their audiences if they are going to communicate to them. For example, as I sit at my typewriter, I am fictionalizing, envisioning my audience as my Mother, catechism teachers, priests, collegians, and seminarians. This audience is a fiction because these people are not reading my material right now nor talking to me about it. When you read what I wrote, you, in turn, have to fictionalize yourself in order to understand me. For example, my frequent use of "you" in reference to my readers invites you to enter into dialogue with me. By sharing personal examples with you, I foster that fiction of dialogue. It is a fiction, you know, since the two of us may be thousands of miles apart as you read this material. Going beyond Ong's analysis, though, I have found that a reader fictionalizes the author. While you are reading my commentary, you are forming an image of me, you are fictionalizing me. Even though you may never have met me, you fictionalize me as of a certain disposition, education, height, etc.

If we apply these insights on image-making to the Pastorals, the scenario goes something like this. The author of the Pastorals has fictionalized his audience and envisioned them as Christians who want to follow Paul in the changed circumstances after his death. Put briefly, the church is experiencing the time of the transition from an apostolic era to a post-apostolic one. (See the General Introduction and the Introduction to 2 Timothy for more detail on the image of transition and loss.) The first readers of the Pastorals fictionalized themselves as Christians living in that post-apostolic era, people seeking guidance on how to follow the apostolic teaching when Paul *the* apostle, had departed. When you stop to think of it, you realize that the situation envisioned for the first readers of the Pastorals is exactly the same situation in which we contemporary readers find ourselves. We are post-apostolic Christians seeking after our roots. A final point. How did the first readers of the Pastorals envision or fictionalize Paul? The author has helped them immeasurably in the formation of their image of Paul by the picture he painted in 2 Tim: Paul is the martyr apostle who practiced his teaching that "if we have died with him, we shall also live with him? (2 Tim 2:11). In living out this teaching, he gave the lie to those who claimed that his teaching meant non-involvement in the human situation. In 1 Tim and Titus the author portrays Paul as *the* apostle who gives directions for all phases of the church's life. By following these directions, the church will be able to cope during the time after Paul's death.

Let me make one further point about image-making. Images are tenacious. Once formed in our minds, they are difficult to dislodge. For example, my image of the late John F. Kennedy is still that of a young, visionary, martyr President even though I know what the revisionist historians say about his poor administrative record and his extramarital undertakings. What image do you have of the Paul who writes the Pastorals? How have you fictionalized, imaged him? Is your image of him drawn from reading his epistles, from catechism classes, from Sunday sermons, or whatever? Should you and I modify the image of Paul to which we tenaciously cling?

So the author of 1 Tim and Titus wants you to envision Paul as *the* apostle who gives guidance for the church as it moves into the future of the post-apostolic era. The author does not depict the Paul who gives this guidance as one who champions ecclesiastical law and order. The careful study of the commentary will show that the church structures enjoined by Paul are actually quite fluid. For example, the author does not describe Paul as laying down one and only one pattern for church leadership. There are elders, and a college of elders, and bishop(s) (See 1 Tim 3:1-7; 5:17-22; Titus 1:5,7-9, passages which frustrate the commentator with a harmonizing bent). The author seems to be saying that in the wake of Paul's death there should be structure to ensure the apostolic teaching, but choose whichever one fits your situation best or devise a new one like the order of widows. Amid this fluidity there are two constants in 1 Tim and Titus. There is the emphasis on sound teaching, and the emphasis on a good conscience, on godliness, on irreproachable conduct. I shall frequently remark on this latter emphasis in the commentary on 1 Tim and Titus.

In resume, before you proceed to study 1 Tim, Titus, and the commentary on them, examine your image of Paul. The Paul who in 1 Tim and Titus gives guidance for church life is not a purveyor of ecclesiastical rigidity, but one who wants to guide the church into a post-apostolic era faithfully and courageously.

PAUL, APOSTLE OF GOD, THE SAVIOR
1 Tim 1:1-2.

1 Paul, an apostle of Christ Jesus by command of God our Savior and of Christ Jesus our hope.

> ²To Timothy, my true child in the faith:
> Grace, mercy, and peace from God the Father and Christ Jesus our Lord.

Paul had begun a Christian style of letter-writing by adapting the Greek model. Thus, he greatly expanded the letter opening which customarily went: A to B, Greeting. The author of the Pastorals is heir to Paul's letter-writing style and adapts it by accentuating Paul as *the* Apostle (verse 1). Pauline fellow-workers, or even the Twelve Apostles, are not in view. Timothy is not the only one addressed by the author. He has entire communities in mind. Notice how the author will end this apparently "personal" letter to Timothy in 6:21 with "Grace be with you," where "you" is plural. See also 2 Tim 4:22: "Grace be with you" (plural), and Titus 3:15: "Grace be with you all." The author of the Pastorals depicts Paul as exhorting Timothy and, through him, the churches.

In speaking about God, the author of the Pastorals employs one of his characteristic titles, Savior, in verse 1 (see also 1 Tim 2:3; 4:10; Titus 1:3; 2:10; 3:4. See also 2 Tim 1:10; Titus 1:4; 2:13; 3:6 where Jesus is given the title "Savior"). It does not seem that Christians called Jesus "Savior" to counteract the growing pagan custom of hailing the emperior as savior. The title "Savior" had strong Old Testament roots, e.g., Is 12:2: "Behold, God is my salvation; I will trust, and will not be afraid; for the Lord God is my strength and my song, and he has become my salvation."

For more detail on the content and function of the prefaces in the Pastorals, see the commentaries on 2 Tim 1:1-2 and Titus 1:1-4.

What Kind of Letters are 1 Timothy and Titus?

In the commentary on 2 Tim 1:1-2 I raised the important question, "What Kind of Letter is 2 Timothy?" As we embark on the commentary on 1 Tim and Titus, I raise a similar question. While requesting that you look at the commentary on 2 Tim 1:1-2 for a more lengthy discussion of the kinds of letters in antiquity, I make the following brief points. 1 Tim and Titus are not "letters home" or "letters to or from a friend." They are exhortatory letters. The author describes Paul, *the* Apostle, as giving his authoritative sanction to the church and household regulations found in these epistles. The author achieves this goal not only by having Paul author these epistles, but also by using imperatives and "must" verbs. These imperatives run through 1 Tim and Titus and clearly show that they are exhortatory. Here is evidence:

First Person Singular Verbs

1 Tim 1:3	—	"I urged"
1 Tim 2:1	—	"I urge"
1 Tim 2:8	—	"I desire"
1 Tim 2:12	—	"I permit"
1 Tim 5:14	—	"So I would have"
1 Tim 5:21	—	"I charge"
Titus 1:5	—	"I directed you"

Second Person Singular Verbs

1 Tim 5:1	—	"Do not rebuke . . . but exhort"
1 Tim 5:3	—	"Honor widows"
1 Tim 5:7	—	"Command this"
1 Tim 5:11	—	"But refuse"
1 Tim 5:19	—	"Never admit"
1 Tim 5:20	—	"Rebuke them"
1 Tim 5:22	—	"Do not be hasty . . . nor participate . . . keep"
Titus 2:1	—	"Teach"
Titus 2:6	—	"Urge"
Titus 3:1	—	"Remind"

Third Person Singular and Plural

1 Tim 2:11	—	"Let a woman learn"
1 Tim 3:10	—	"Let them be tested first . . . let them serve"
1 Tim 3:12	—	"Let deacons be"
1 Tim 5:4	—	"Let them first learn"

1 Tim 5:9	—	"Let a widow be enrolled"
1 Tim 5:16	—	"Let her assist them"
1 Tim 5:17	—	"Let the elders . . . be considered worthy"
1 Tim 6:1	—	"Let all . . . regard"
1 Tim 6:2	—	"Let them not be disrespectful . . . let them serve" (translation by author)

Impersonal "Must" or "Ought" Verbs

1 Tim 3:2	—	"Now a bishop must be"
1 Tim 3:7	—	"He must be"
1 Tim 3:15	—	"How one ought to behave"
Titus 1:7	—	"Must be blameless"

This evidence shows how the author places the authority of the Apostle Paul behind the regulations contained in these two epistles. The student could profitably contrast this usage with Polycarp of Smyrna's Letter to the Philippians 4:1-6:2, where no finite verb occurs, and Polycarp does not use his authority to sanction the traditional material on the qualities of deacons, presbyters, widows, etc.

In brief, 1 Tim and Titus do not fall into the category of "a letter to a friend." They are exhortatory letters to churches.

THE MERCY OF CHRIST JESUS ENABLES CHRISTIANS TO LOVE AND BUILD UP SOCIETY.
1 Tim 1:3-20.

> 3As I urged you when I was going to Macedonia, remain at Ephesus that you may charge certain persons not to teach any different doctrine, 4nor to occupy themselves with myths and endless genealogies which promote speculations rather than the divine training that is in faith; 5whereas the aim of our charge is love that issues from a pure heart and a good conscience and sincere faith. 6Certain persons by swerving from these have wandered away into vain discussion, 7desiring to be teachers of the law, without understanding either what

they are saying or the things about which they make assertions.

⁸Now we know that the law is good, if any one uses it lawfully, ⁹understanding this, that the law is not laid down for the just but for the lawless and disobedient, for the ungodly and sinners, for the unholy and profane, for murderers of fathers and murderers of mothers, for manslayers, ¹⁰immoral persons, sodomites, kidnapers, liars, perjurers, and whatever else is contrary to sound doctrine, ¹¹in accordance with the glorious gospel of the blessed God with which I have been entrusted.

¹²I thank him who has given me strength for this, Christ Jesus our Lord, because he judged me faithful by appointing me to his service, ¹³though I formerly blasphemed and persecuted and insulted him; but I received mercy because I had acted ignorantly in unbelief, ¹⁴and the grace of our Lord overflowed for me with the faith and love that are in Christ Jesus. ¹⁵The saying is sure and worthy of full acceptance, that Christ Jesus came into the world to save sinners. And I am the foremost of sinners; ¹⁶but I received mercy for this reason, that in me, as the foremost, Jesus Christ might display his perfect patience for an example to those who were to believe in him for eternal life. ¹⁷To the King of ages, immortal, invisible, the only God, be honor and glory for ever and ever. Amen.

¹⁸This charge I commit to you, Timothy, my son, in accordance with the prophetic utterances which pointed to you, that inspired by them you may wage the good warfare, ¹⁹holding faith and a good conscience. By rejecting conscience, certain persons have made shipwreck of their faith, ²⁰among them Hymenaeus and Alexander whom I have delivered to Satan that they may learn not to blaspheme.

One day while shopping, I fell into conversation with a lady. During the course of our conversation I mentioned that I was writing a book and had come to a particularly difficult section. My tendency in the past would have been to skip over that section and deal with an easier one—almost hoping that the difficult section would evaporate. In my old age, I told her, I have learned to attack the difficult section right away. By doing that, I save time and do a better job. To my words of wisdom, she remarked, that she does the same thing in her professional work as a seamstress. She tackles the jobs she dislikes first.

We have come to a section which is particularly difficult to interpret because, for example, verses 3-5 do not form a complete sentence, "law" seems to be used in two different senses in verses 7 and 8, and the clauses in verses 10b-11 dangle without any clear indication of what they modify. But we cannot put this difficult section on the back burner, quietly hoping that by the time we return to it, it will have disappeared. We chip away at the difficulties of this section from four directions.

Key Message of the Section

In the "Introduction to 1 Timothy and Titus" I called your attention to a leitmotif of these letters: they stress good behavior. By their good conduct Christians will show one another and their fellow citizens that their faith is true. This section lays the foundations for the admonitions on good conduct to be found in 2:1-3:13. The "then"/therefore of 2:1 links the material of this section with those admonitions. Put in other words, since Christians should be about good behavior (1:3-20), these are the types of conduct in which they should engage (2:1-3:13). This observation will become even clearer if we look at three points.

First, notice how frequently the vocabulary of this section deals with conduct: "love that issues from a pure heart and a good conscience and sincere faith" (verse 5); "the law is not laid down for the just but for the lawless" (verse 9); "and I am the foremost of sinners; but I received mercy" (verses

15-16); "holding faith and a good conscience" (verse 19). Through his commands to Timothy the author wants to ensure that his communities live according to sound doctrine, that is, doctrine which promotes the moral health of individual Christians and of society.

Second, let's rescue the "dangling" clause of verse 11 by maintaining that it modifies all that precedes it. That is, a life of love is in accord with the gospel whereas vain speculations are not (verses 3-5). Grievous, society-destroying sins like the murder of one's mother and kidnapping are not in accord with Paul's gospel (verses 6-9). Paul's gospel does not issue in a book of abstract truths, but in teaching which is productive of moral growth (verse 10; the adjective "sound" in the phrase "sound doctrine" should be construed much like the usage in the idiom: "they arrived safe and sound").

Third, Paul is the prime example of God's will to promote healthy moral life (verses 12-17). We might capture this aspect of the author's truth by paraphrasing the "sure saying" of verse 15: "Christ Jesus did not come into the world to make us sinners." Christ Jesus' mercy and perfect patience transform sinners into "just" people (see verse 9). For more detail on the function of Paul's example in this section, see below. (For more data on "sure sayings," see the commentary on 2 Tim 2:1-13.)

In summary, the key message of this passage is that Paul's gospel and example promote good conduct and lead to love which stems from a heart that is singleminded, a conscience that has no guilt on it, and from a faith that practices what it confesses.

How the Author Argues in This Section

It is vital to recall that the author is writing an exhortatory letter. Even in passages like this where he attacks opponents, his aim is exhortation, not apologetic. As he does in 2 Tim 2:14-26, the author contrasts exhortations with references to the teachings of the opponents; he also argues by means of link-words. Let us look at his method of argumentation in detail:

1:3a	—	exhortation to Timothy to *charge* certain persons
1:3b-4	—	the opponents are involved in myths
1:5	—	the aim of our *charge* is love, not speculation
1:6-7	—	certain persons have swerved from love and good conscience, the aim of our *charge*, and want to be teachers of the *law*
1:8-10	—	the *law* is for sinners
1:11	—	what I have *charged* you is in accordance with the *gospel* with which I have been entrusted
1:12-17	—	in the person of Paul, Christ Jesus shows the nature of the *gospel*: sinners are saved.
1:18-19a	—	be faithful to your *charge* to fight opponents of faith and *conscience*
1:19b-20	—	examples of those who rejected *conscience*

While giving exhortations to Timothy, the author attacks a group within the church which stresses law "without understanding either what they are saying or the things about which they make assertions" (verse 7). In the next part we investigate the nature of this group.

The Jewish Component in the Heresy Combatted in the Pastorals

In the commentary on 2 Tim 2:14-26 I devoted considerable attention to the nature of the heresy combatted in the Pastorals. This section provides us with the opportunity to add a few more brush strokes to the sketch I painted there.

Because the author refers to "law" in verses 7-9, most commentators rightly interpret the "myths and endless genealogies" of verse 4 as references to Jewish interpretations of the Old Testament. This view is supported by two parallel passages in Titus: "Therefore rebuke them sharply, that they may be sound in the faith, instead of giving heed to Jewish myths" (1:13-14); "but avoid stupid controversies, genealogies, dissensions, and quarrels over the law, for they are unprofitable and futile" (3:9).

In correcting the opponents' view of "law," the author gives "law" another meaning. Verses 3-7 provide the view of the opponents who want to be teachers of the law. For them the law is the Torah or first five books of the Old Testament. In verses 8-10 the author sets them clear by giving his own definition of law. In doing so, he draws upon Pauline tradition: "So the law is holy, and the commandment is holy and just and good" (Rom 7:12); "Now if I do what I do not want, I agree that the law is good" (Rom 7:16). But then, having introduced this general principle from the Pauline tradition, the author moves along his own path of understanding and defines "law" as the moral teachings accepted by Christians. Such moral teachings are not laid down for the Christian who is made just by God's grace (see verses 9,13,16), but for those who would ruin society by their heinous conduct and would eliminate love from the face of the earth (verses 9-10). Put another way, the author of the Pastorals is saying to the would-be teachers of the law: Don't give us any of your speculations about the Torah, give us law-abiding people. If your speculations do not build up society and Christian community, cease and desist from them.

In the above paragraph I have given the gist of the author's case against the opponents. If we dig a little deeper, we will see how complex the issue really is. The main issue is how to interpret the Old Testament. In 2 Tim 3:15 the author provides one key of interpretation, Christ Jesus: "the sacred writings which are able to instruct you for salvation through faith in Christ Jesus." I will give you two examples from Jewish and Christian materials to show you other ways of interpreting the Old Testament.

In a first century B.C. work called *Jubilees* the author speculates about creation and genealogies among other things, as he rewrites the book of Genesis, the first book of the Torah. Here are two representative passages which may help you to appreciate what the author means by "myths and endless genealogies" (verse 4):

> And the angel of the presence spoke to Moses according to the word of the Lord, saying: Write the complete history of the creation, how in six days the Lord God finished all his works and all that he created, and kept Sabbath on the seventh day and hallowed it for all ages, and appointed it as a sign for all his works. For on the first day he created the heavens which are above and the earth and the waters and all the spirits which serve before him—the angels of the presence, and the angels of sanctification, and the angels of the spirit of the winds ... (2:1-2).

> And in the eleventh jubilee Jared took to himself a wife, and her name was Baraka, the daughter of Rasujal, a daughter of his father's brother, in the fourth week of this jubilee, and she bore him a son in the fifth week, in the fourth year of the jubilee, and he called his name Enoch. And he was the first among men that are born on earth who learnt writing and knowledge and wisdom and who wrote down the signs of heaven according to the order of their months in a book, that men might know the seasons of the years according to the order of their separate months. And he was the first to write a testimony, and he testified to the sons of men among the generations of the earth, and recounted the weeks of the jubilees ... And what was and what will be he saw in a vision of his sleep, saw and understood everything, and wrote his testimony, and placed the testimony on earth for all the children of men and for their generations (4:16-19; from the translation in R.H. Charles, ed., *The Apocrypha and Pseudepigrapha of the Old Testament II*).

In these two excerpts you can see how the author added the creation of the angels to the Genesis story of the creation of the first day. To the Genesis account of Enoch's birth much has been added. Enoch was the seer par excellence. From the perspective of the people who wrote and used

Jubilees such additions were profitable. From the perspective of the author of the Pastorals the key question is whether these additions lead to better moral behavior or foster dangerous curiosity.

As Ignatius of Antioch, a contemporary of the author of the Pastorals, travelled through Asia Minor on his way to Rome and martyrdom, he encountered different Jewish groups. Against some of them Ignatius held to the principle that the Old Testament is to be interpreted by means of the revelation of Jesus Christ: "Be not led astray by strange doctrines or by old myths which are profitless. For if we are living until now according to Judaism, we confess that we have not received grace. For the divine prophets lived according to Jesus Christ." (*Ignatius to the Magnesians* 8:1-2; Loeb translation modified). Ignatius' key to the Old Testament is Jesus Christ; all other keys are myths.

These two examples open a door to the different ways of interpreting the Old Testament which were current when the Pastorals were written. The author of the Pastorals condemns speculations like those found in *Jubilees*. He seems to be like Ignatius of Antioch, who maintains that views contrary to his own are a graceless "living according to Judaism." His main contention against the would-be "teachers of the law" is that their speculations about the Torah miss the whole point of the Gospel, which is to promote love.

In conclusion, there is a Jewish component to the heresy combatted in the Pastorals. The communities of the Pastorals were being disturbed by Jewish Christians who championed in-depth speculations on the Torah. See the General Introduction to the Pastorals for more detail about the nature of this heresy.

The Image of Paul, Witness to the Power of the Gospel of Mercy

We have come to our final probe into the difficulties of this section. In the "Introduction to 2 Timothy" and "Introduction to 1 Timothy and Titus" I underscored the importance of the image of Paul in the theology of the Pastorals.

Verses 12-17 add another facet to the image of the suffering Paul, *the* apostle, who authoritatively issues the regulations contained in 1 Tim and Titus. Behind the messages of the Pastorals stands the authority of a Paul whose very life is proof positive of the power of God's mercy. In terms which Paul would not use (contrast Phil 3:5) Paul's past is described as singularly wretched (verse 13). But he is what he is because of overflowing grace. The foremost sinner has become the foremost example of Christ Jesus' mercy. This view of Paul's conversion is very similar to that which the second century A.D. *Epistle of Barnabas* provides of the apostles: "But when he chose out his own Apostles who were to preach his Gospel, he chose those who were iniquitous above all sin to show that 'he came not to call the righteous but sinners,'—then he manifested himself as God's Son" (5:9; Loeb translation).

The "sure saying" of verse 15 seems to be built upon Lk 19:10: "For the Son of man came to seek and to save the lost." This sure saying, which stems from a creed commonly professed by first century Christians, is interpreted by the life of Paul. Just as Paul's life interpreted the creedal materials of 2 Tim 2:8-13, it does so here too (see also 1 Tim 2:1-7). In the church of the Pastorals the Pauline tradition and commonly accepted Christian creeds do not exist side by side, but mutually interpret one another.

Verses 12-17 conclude with a prayer. Prayer is the most appropriate response to all that Paul has received from Christ Jesus. It is the response of the Christian communities of the Pastorals which draw hope for God's mercy from the way God intervened in the life of Paul, the foremost sinner. Honor and glory forever to the God who has bestowed upon us the blessings of Paul's directions and life.

THE CHURCH'S RELATIONSHIP WITH SOCIETY.
1 Tim 2:1-7.

2 First of all, then, I urge that supplications, prayers, intercessions, and thanksgivings be made for all men, [2]for kings and all who are in high positions, that we may lead a quiet and peaceable life, godly and respectful in every way. ³This is good, and it is acceptable in the sight of God our Savior, ⁴who desires all men to be saved and to come to the knowledge of the truth. ⁵For there is one God, and there is one mediator between God and men, the man Christ Jesus, ⁶who gave himself as a ransom for all, the testimony to which was borne at the proper time. ⁷For this I was appointed a preacher and apostle (I am telling the truth, I am not lying), a teacher of the Gentiles in faith and truth.

We have come to a very rich passage, whose treasures we will explore from five perspectives.

How This Passage is Related to Its Context

If you are like me, you have a tendency to approach a passage like this concordance-style. That is, you check in the concordance under "rulers," light upon this passage, and study it for what it can contribute to your immediate concerns. You do not see how it relates to its context and consequently fail to spot some additional facets of its beauty and wisdom.

In 1 Tim 1:3-20 the author announced his theme that sound doctrine must issue in righteous conduct. In 2:1-7 he spells out what righteous conduct means with regard to prayer and rulers; in 2:8-15 he will detail the conduct expected of men and women, husbands and wives. The moral qualities of church leaders will be his chief concern in 3:1-13 as well as in the rest of this epistle. This is the broad context in which 2:1-7 occurs. If we ask about its immediate context, then we focus on 3:14-16, for in these verses the author informs us of his reasons for giving the instructions of 2:1-3:13. The conduct he describes in 2:1-7 is part and parcel of "how one ought to behave in the household of God, which is the church of the living God, the pillar and bulwark of the truth" (3:15). 1 Tim 2:1-7 delineates what is expected of those whose conduct flows from the truth they confess.

The universalism of 2:1-7 is bolstered by the universalism of the hymn found in 3:16: "preached *among the nations*." The world-affirming attitude of 2:1-7 is supported by "believed on *in the world*" of 3:16.

Let me make my point in a slightly different way. In the "Introduction to 1 Timothy and Titus" I emphasized that the author uses the authority of Paul to sanction the ecclesiastical and household regulations he borrowed from different traditions. In this section we begin to see how the author also uses creedal materials (see 2:4-6 and 3:16) to support his exhortations.

To recapitulate, try to view each set of exhortations found in 1 Tim and Titus within their contexts. This discipline will give you rich insights into how the author draws inferences for conduct from creedal statements like "God desires all to be saved" (verse 4).

The Signal Importance of Prayer

The first impression we may get from reading and studying the Pastorals is that they are drab and dreary, somber and sober. But the study of a passage like this should help both you and me to correct that impression. "First of all" (verse 1) means "of prime importance." In the author's view of Christian life, prayer is of signal importance. To support this observation I would invite you to read through the Pastorals once again. It won't take long; the epistles are short. Jot down how often the author depicts Paul praying, exhorting to prayer, or using creedal materials and hymns, which came from liturgical celebrations. For example, look at 1 Tim 1:12: "I thank him," and 1 Tim 1:17: "To the King of ages," and 1 Tim 3:16: "Great indeed, we *confess*, is the mystery of our religion," which is followed by a liturgical hymn.

The author of the Pastorals and the communities of faith around him arrived at the regulations for conduct recorded in 1 Tim and Titus by reflecting, in prayer, on the core tenets of the faith they celebrated in the liturgy. In the next part I will take you backstage to see how the author has derived rules for conduct from a creed which proclaimed God's universal salvific will.

God's Will-To-Save Embraces All

The word "all" dominates this passage; see verses 1,2,4, and 6. I make two points. First, gnostic opponents may have taught that salvation was limited to some few elect and that "knowledge of the truth" is not open to all people (verse 4). They may have taught that there are more gods than the one God and more mediators than the one mediator, the man Christ Jesus (verse 5). Against such teaching the author underlines God's universal salvific will in verse 6 by citing a universalized version of Mk 10:45: "For the Son of man also came not to be served but to serve, and to give his life as a ransom for many." To this commonly accepted Christian creed the author adds the weight of Paul's authority. "For this," that is, to proclaim God's universal salvific will, Paul has been appointed to move outside the confines of Judaism into the regions of the "nations" (this is a more accurate translation than the narrower "Gentiles"; the same Greek word is translated by "nations" in 3:16). See the commentary on 2 Tim 2:14-26 for more detail on the gnostic element in the heresy combatted in the Pastorals.

Secondly, to us who live some eighteen centuries after the author of the Pastorals, it may be self-evident that we should pray for all people. But as we have just seen, it was not self-evident to the gnostic opponents the author combats. Prayer for all people "is good, and it is acceptable in the sight of God our Savior" who wills the salvation of all (verses 3-4). This example of the author's way of inferring concrete conduct from creeds is not an isolated case. See for example, how the detailed regulations for the household found in Titus 2:1-10 are supported by the creed-like materials of 2:11-14. See in particular how verse 11 begins with "for" and demonstrates how the conduct enjoined in 2:1-10 stems from the kerygma articulated in 2:11-14.

The Author Does Not Enjoin One Rigid Set of Regulations

To return to the image of concordance study with which I began the observations of this section, I would say that if you looked up "rulers" you would find not only 1 Tim 2:2 listed, but also Titus 3:1. But then as you studied the two passages, you would notice that they do not make exactly the same points nor are they motivated by the same creed. And as you would study other words in the Pastorals like "bishop," "elders," and "women," you would find the same thing to be true. The author is not consistent in what he says about the duties of these people. He draws from various traditions within the churches and invites his readers to run with whatever structures meet their needs, provided that these structures foster sound doctrine and good conduct.

The Question of How The Church Relates to Society - 1 Tim 2:2

Let me clarify the question of how the author of the Pastorals views the church's relationship to society by contrasting his views with those of Paul and those of the gnostic opponents he combats. For the latter, the world is not to be viewed positively. The less the Christian gets involved in matter, the better. See the commentaries on 2 Tim 2:14-26 and 1 Tim 4:1-16 for more data on this aspect of the gnostic heresy. Paul's view was to take obedience to civil authorities as an obvious obligation, and not to look upon societal structures in much detail (see Rom 13:1-12 and especially 1 Cor 7:29-31). The passage from 1 Cor bears full quotation:

> I mean, brethren, the appointed time has grown very short; from now on, let those who have wives live as though they had none, and those who mourn as though they were not mourning, and those who rejoice as though they were not rejoicing, and those who buy as though they had no goods, and those who deal with the world as though they had no dealings with it. For the form of this world is passing away.

Because of his view of Christ's imminent parousia Paul did not take time to figure out in a more detailed way the Christian's relationship with the world. It was the task of those who championed the Pauline tradition at the turn of the first Christian century to deal with the question of the Christian's relationship to society. One such champion was the author of the Pastorals.

In verse 2 the author of the Pastorals views society's political powers positively and prays that the peace they bring and maintain will benefit the Christian mission to all. Seen from this perspective, verse 2 does not conflict with the persecution situation I proposed as the background for 2 Tim. A host of commentators have seen the author's goal of a "quiet and peaceful life" (verse 2) as part of his "bourgeois" or middle-class ethic, which does not challenge the established order, but is eager to live by its norms. This viewpoint is expressed very sharply by J. H. Houlden:

> By the Pastoral Epistles, we have moved to a more settled perspective, to what we might call the first news-paper-reading generation of churchmen, those aware of some responsibility for society and interested in its affairs . . . . Yet of course, if bourgeois, then certainly *petit* bourgeois. The interest of this writer's circle is not to take part in public affairs or to direct them, but to *lead a quiet and peaceable life*, and, we may suppose, not to distinguish too keenly between good emperors and bad, but to support the existing powers so long as this mini-mum condition is fulfilled . . . . What churchmen can provide is prayer not criticism (*The Pastoral Epistles*, pp. 64-65).

Houlden's observations must be taken with utmost seriousness. As the church of the Pastorals settled down in the world, it adapted many norms for its life from the bourgeois standards of contemporary society. In the re-maining sections of the commentary on 1 Tim and Titus I will have ample opportunity to show you evidence of how such adaptation transpired. The Christians who did the adapting and their successors have to remember that these norms did not come down from heaven. They avoid absolutizing the way society at one period of time thought it was best to do something, e.g., bishops should be husbands of one wife; wives should be subordinate to their husbands. A contemporary example will illuminate this point further. The church's theology and regulations on marriage draw heavily upon society's view of marriage. Now that the best thinking in society is moving away from a contractual model of marriage to a personalist one, the church is adjusting its theology of marriage. Thus, the language of covenant, fidelity, and conjugal love is replacing that of the rights of the married partners to one another's body.

Houlden is correct that the stance which the author of the Pastorals takes toward society may involve the church in praying for society, but not in criticizing it. To get us on the Pastorals' wavelength, recall some of the storms which recently raged in the U.S. church. There was much agitation in the church over the issue of whether the U.S. government's war policies in Vietnam may have been civilly correct, but morally wrong. Abortion may be allowed by civil law, but be morally wrong. Indeed, the "quiet and peaceful life" the author of the Pastorals prays for may have deleterious consequences. We might even be good citizens, but poor Christians.

Forewarned of the deficiencies of the author's middle-class ethic, let us see what positive lessons we can learn from his world-affirming attitude. His is not simply a conformist or "bourgeois ethics." The society of his time cared little for widows, yet the "faith" of his community— nurtured by the Jesus tradition of care for the outcasts?— determined that these outcasts should be cared for. The author lays down a principle which is startling in its insistence on the social obligations of one's faith: "If any one does not provide for his relatives, and especially for his own family, he has *disowned the faith* and is worse than an unbeliever" (1 Tim 5:8). Seen from another angle, the author is not afraid to take the risk of moving from the level of the general principle—care of outcasts—to its application in a concrete situation. Once he moves away from that general principle with which almost everyone agrees and moves to a secondary or tertiary level of application, he may not be able to persuade all of the obligation of doing what he enjoins. But his vision will not allow him to let that general principle float around in heavenly, but irrelevant abstraction.

The author presents us with a vision of the Christian's relationship to society. He forms people who are willing to take a big risk in living the Christian life in the midst of a pluralistic society. They meditate on the life of Paul and on the creeds they profess to see what implications they have for daily life. In breaking through the secure thought world of a sect, they strive to be a leaven in the entire world. In their hearts joy and anxiety alternate: joy that more people understand and live the gospel in changed circumstances; anxiety that one may have compromised the gospel for the sake of adaptation to a changed world. Such are the emotions that pulse through those who envision Christianity as a universal religion.

THE HUMAN SITUATION IS THE ARENA IN WHICH SALVATION IS PLAYED.
1 Tim 2:8-15.

> 8I desire then that in every place the men should pray, lifting holy lands without anger or quarreling; 9also that women should adorn themselves modestly and sensibly in seemly apparel, not with braided hair or gold or pearls or costly attire 10but by good deeds, as befits women who profess religion. 11Let a woman learn in silence with all submissiveness. 12I permit no woman to teach or to have authority over men; she is to keep silent. 13For Adam was formed first, then Eve; 14and Adam was not deceived, but the woman was deceived and

became a transgressor. [15]Yet woman will be saved through bearing children, if she continues in faith and love and holiness, with modesty.

Sometime back I mentioned to one of my younger confreres that when I was in grade school, we did not have television. Full of amazement, he gasped, "So that's what it was like in those days!" As I approach this passage, I realize that you and I come to it with our twentieth-century views of marriage and as participants or observers of the contemporary movements for women's liberation and ordination. These are the glasses through which we view this passage. But as an exegete and commentator, I must set this passage within its contexts and ask: "What were things like back in those days?" As we put on the glasses of those days, we will be amazed at what we see. We treat this passage in its different contexts.

The Immediate Context of This Passage

This passage continues the directives of "how one ought to behave in the household of God . . . the pillar and bulwark of the truth" (3:15). In a style characteristic of exhortatory writing the author abruptly moves from admonitions on the content of prayer (2:1-7) to admonitions on the manner of praying (2:8-10). He uses the catchword "all"/"every" to connect this passage with the preceding section; see "all" in verse 6 and "every" in verse 8.

In verse 8 the author adapts a tradition which stressed the necessity of matching ritual with righteous conduct. Verses 9-10 lay down the injunction that women should adorn themselves with the joyful countenance and bearing of a person who delights in doing good deeds (see 1 Pt 3:1-6 for a similar admonition). Verses 11-12 are very stern and occur almost without warning. Verses 13-15 provide a rationale for these stern injunctions. Two points emerge from a closer analysis of verses 13-15. First, "woman" (a generic term in Greek) should probably be translated as "wife" in these verses. Secondly, the phrase "through bearing children" is key and indicates that the heretics' teaching that marriage is forbidden (1 Tim 4:3) stands behind this passage. But with this observation we are on the brink of discussing the next context in which this passage must be viewed.

The Context of This Passage in the Pastorals

The stern character of the admonitions in verses 11-12 and the rationale of salvation through child-bearing (verse 15) lead me to check the larger context of all three Pastoral Epistles. In the commentary on 2 Tim 3:1-9 I mentioned that the heretics, combatted in the Pastorals, had success among women. As we see in the commentary on 1 Tim 4:1-16, the heretics forbade marriage (1 Tim 4:3). In Titus 2:4-5 the author enjoins the older women to train "the younger women to love their husbands and children, to be sensible, chaste, domestic, kind, and submissive to their husbands, *that the word of God may not be discredited.*" From these three passages in the larger context of the Pastorals I would conclude that the heretics had won over women who joined them as teachers. Their message was that marriage, sexual intercourse, and procreation are evil. Such teaching shocked both the Christian and non-Christian communities and led to the discrediting of the word of God among the pagans. Let me bolster my conclusion by moving to a new context, a context which will provide interpretative parallels to the teachings of the heretics combatted in the Pastorals.

The Context of This Passage in Light of Gnostic Teaching

We in the Roman Catholic tradition are generally quite comfortable in theory and in practice with the teaching that creation, marriage, sexual intercourse, and procreation are good. But the security of that teaching was the result of long and hard-fought battles in the history of the church. At the time of the Pastorals a number of gnostics did not look favorably on creation, marriage, sexual intercourse, and procreation. One such person was Saturnilus (ca. 130

A.D.). St. Irenaeus (*Adversus Haereses* 1.24.2) provides us with this thumbnail sketch of Saturnilus' teaching. I have italicized the salient parts:

> The Savior he (Saturnilus) assumed to be unbegotten, incorporeal, and without form, but appeared in semblance as a man. The God of the Jews, he says, was one of the angels; and because all the archons wanted to destroy the Father, Christ came for the destruction of the God of the Jews and the salvation of those who believe in him; these are they who have the spark of life in them. He was first to say that two kinds of men had been moulded by the angels, the one wicked, the other good. And since the demons helped the wicked, the Savior came for the destruction of the wicked men and demons, and the salvation of the good. *Marriage and procreation, he says, are of Satan.* Many of his followers *abstain also from animal food*, and through this feigned continence they lead many astray (translation in W. Foerster, *Gnosis I*, p. 41).

The gnostic teaching combatted in the Pastorals was something like that espoused by Saturnilus. Against such teaching the author of the Pastorals says that the order of creation, which includes the bearing and rearing of children, is not contrary to the order of salvation. Christian wives will be able to work out their salvation by bearing children. This salvation is not automatic, though. Wives must persevere "in faith and love and holiness, with modesty" (verse 15). Put another way, the bearing of children is not evil; it is a human arena in which salvation is played.

Not only men like Saturnilus, but also women taught these gnostic doctrines. There are very illuminating passages in the second century *Acts of Paul*. In one passage Paul is accused of teaching: "But he deprives young men of wives and maidens of husbands, saying, 'Otherwise there is no resurrection for you, except you remain chaste and do not defile the flesh, but keep it pure'" (paragraph 12).

The encratite Paul convinces the engaged lady Thecla of his teaching, and both are accused before the governor who asks Thecla: "'Why do you not marry Thamyris according to the law of the Iconians?'" (paragraph 20). After detailing Thecla's wondrous exploits, the *Acts of Paul* concludes on this note: "And when she had borne this witness she went away to Seleucia; and after enlightening many with the word of God she slept with a noble sleep" (paragraph 43; modified translation of E. Hennecke; W. Schneemelcher, eds., *New Testament Apocrypha II*). The woman Thecla teaches the message that marriage is wrong and that those who marry will have no resurrection. And this teaching scandalizes non-Christians, for it is not "according to the law of the Iconians." (See Titus 2:4-5 in which the author instructs that the wives' failure to be submissive to their husbands will cause the Christian name to be discredited among the pagans.)

In resume, the passages about Saturnilus and Thecla provide us with a backdrop from "back in those days." Against this backdrop it is easier to situate the harsh admonitions of verses 11-12 and to explain "bearing of children" in verse 15. We turn now to still another context - the Pauline tradition - in our search for light on this passage.

The Context of the Pauline Tradition
1 Cor 14:33b-36 is very similar to 1 Tim 2:11-12 and seems to be its source. Allow me to quote 1 Cor 14:33b-36 in full:

> As in all the churches of the saints, the women should keep silence in the churches. For they are not permitted to speak, but should be subordinate, as even the law says. If there is anything they desire to know, let them ask their husbands at home. For it is shameful for a woman to speak in church. What! Did the word of God originate with you, or are you the only ones it has reached?

To meet his need of combatting women teachers of gnostic persuasion, the author borrowed from this passage. "For they are not permitted to speak" was too vague for him. He specified "to speak" to mean "to teach." By adapting this Pauline tradition, the author used the authority of Paul in still another way to combat gnostic women who were teaching in his churches. (It is impossible in this commentary to enter into a discussion of Paul's view of women. See my article, "The Role of Women according to Jesus and the Early Church," in C. Stuhlmueller, ed., *Women and Priesthood*, pp. 47-57, for my views on this complex subject).

Having worked our way through the various ancient contexts of our passage, we are now ready to investigate its contemporary context.

The Contemporary Context of Our Passage

In this section I don my hat of biblical theologian and comment on the relevance of this passage for today.

As I view this passage in its multiple ancient contexts, I see that it has nothing to say against the ordination of women to the priesthood. For the threat of gnostic female teachers in the pulpits and classrooms of the church has obviously passed. And with the passing of that threat, so too has passed the validity of the harsh injunctions of verses 11-12. The church at large for centuries has implicitly maintained this interpretation, for there are thousands of women teachers in the church. The trustworthiness of such teachers also tells against the author's reading of the Genesis account of the Fall (see verse 14). Eve does not typify wives' gullibility and hence untrustworthiness as teachers.

The major contribution of this passage to the contemporary situation is its positive view of creation. The author insists that creation, matter, marriage, sexual intercourse, procreation are good. He preserved the Pauline tradition in the face of gnostics who contended that creation was the work of an inferior god. We are heirs of the author's positive view of creation and thank him for teaching us that "everything created by God is good, and nothing is to be rejected if it is received with thanksgiving" (1 Tim 4:4).

CHURCH LEADERS MUST BE GOOD HUMAN BEINGS, WHO HOLD THE MYSTERY OF FAITH WITH A CLEAR CONSCIENCE.
1 Tim 3:1-13.

3 The saying is sure: If any one aspires to the office of bishop, he desires a noble task. [2]Now a bishop must be above reproach, the husband of one wife, temperate, sensible, dignified, hospitable, an apt teacher, [3]no drunkard, not violent but gentle, not quarrelsome, and no lover of money. [4]He must manage his own household well, keeping his children submissive and respectful in every way; [5]for if a man does not know how to manage his own household, how can he care for God's church? [6]He must not be a recent convert, or he may be puffed up with conceit and fall into the condemnation of the devil; [7]moreover he must be well thought of by outsiders, or he may fall into reproach and the snare of the devil.

[8]Deacons likewise must be serious, not double-tongued, not addicted to much wine, not greedy for gain; [9]they must hold the mystery of the faith with a clear conscience. [10]And let them also be tested first; then if they prove themselves blameless let them serve as deacons. [11]The women likewise must be serious, no slanderers, but temperate, faithful in all things. [12]Let deacons be the husband of one wife, and let them manage their children and their households well; [13]for those who serve well as deacons gain a good standing for themselves and also great confidence in the faith which is in Christ Jesus.

Some years back ten first-year seminarians and I were interviewing a fifty-five year old pastor. Our subject was priestly ministry. He concluded his answer to one question with, "He's a good priest." When I asked him what he meant by the phrase "a good priest," he paused and then said: "Twenty years ago I thought that 'a good priest' was the one who always had his books balanced, who ran an efficient plant, who provided his parishioners with a full schedule of Masses and confessions. Now I think differently.

'A good priest' is a man of deep prayer and compassion, who considers people more important than buildings, who cares for the poor and needy." This pastor's concepts of priestly ministry had changed over twenty years. And both concepts he had of the priest were products of their times. It should not be surprising, then, that the "requirements" laid down for bishops, deacons, and deaconnesses in this section are different than ours or even different than those of 1 Tim 5:17-22 and Titus 1:5-9. Each is a product of its time and situation. I make five observations on this section.

An Overview of the Passage

First, a word of caution. Both you and I must beware of reading our contemporary understanding of bishop and deacon into this passage. This passage presents us with a view of these offices in an early stage of their development. Second, a word about the structure and nature of the passage. The "sure saying" of verse 1 is specified by a list of moral qualities the bishop must have (verses 2-7). This list has been adapted from contemporary societal norms. Deacons are required to have almost the same moral qualities as the bishop (verses 8-10, 12-13). A brief verse is dedicated to the moral requirements of a deaconess (verse 11). The entire passage consists of loosely connected exhortatory materials about church leaders. Third, a word about what the passage does not say. Since this exhortatory passage stresses the moral qualities prerequisite in different church leaders, it does not provide information on many other points. For example, it does not tell us very much about what these church leaders did; it does not tell us about the role of the Holy Spirit or of ordination in the lives of these leaders.

Adaptation of Societal Norms

Commentators have often pointed out that the moral qualities required in these church leaders are not distinctive. All Christians should have them. We could even go a step further and say that these qualities are those the standards of the time required of a good human being. Let me give you two illustrations of the general character of these moral qualities.

First, in their commentary M. Dibelius and H. Conzelmann cite the qualities which Onosander required of a general in the army:

> I believe, then, that we must choose a general, not because of noble birth as priests are chosen, nor because of wealth as the superintendents of the gymnasia, but because he is temperate, self-restrained, vigilant, frugal, hardened to labor, alert, free from avarice, neither too young nor too old, indeed a father of children if possible, a ready speaker, and a man with a good reputation. The general must be temperate in order that he may not be so distracted by the pleasures of the body as to neglect the consideration of matters of the highest importance . . .
> (*The Pastoral Epistles*, pp. 158-59).

These qualities, while not exactly the same as those required of the church leaders in 1 Tim 3:1-13, are sufficiently similar to point up how non-distinctive the moral qualities required of church leaders are.

Second, verses 5 and 12 draw upon the model of the ideal "father of the household." The father exercised responsibility for wives, children, slaves, and the making of wealth (for more detail on "household" see the commentary on 1 Tim 3:14-16). Creon in Sophocles' *Antigone* gives voice to the ideal which lies behind verses 5 and 12: "If thus I nurse rebellion in my house, shall not I foster mutiny without? For whoso rules his household worthily, will prove in civic matters no less wise" (lines 658-661 in Loeb translation). The author of the Pastorals adapts this bit of Greek wisdom as normative of his church leaders.

From the above two illustrations I draw these conclusions. First, the church leaders had to measure up to the standards expected of people in similarly important positions in contemporary society. Second, in antiquity, and as a matter of fact until the late eighteenth century, there was little room given to individuality and creativity. People followed role models and ideal types. In the words of K. J. Weintraub:

> All such ideals share certain formal characteristics. They prescribe for the individual certain substantive personality traits, certain values, virtues, and attitudes. They embody specific life-styles into which to fit the self. They offer man a script for his life, and only in the unprescribed interstitial spaces is there room for idiosyncrasy . . . . But the all-important point is that, despite all variation, the man who sought to follow such models saw virtue in approaching and fulfilling an exemplary way of being human while placing very little value on idiosyncratic differences - if at all (*The Value of the Individual.* pp. xv-xvi).

Rather than marvel at the wholesale borrowing the church engaged in to arrive at the moral qualities requisite in its leaders, we should marvel to what extent it was able to creatively adapt these ideal types and role models (see verses 5b-7,9,13): Church leaders are fine human beings who hold the mystery of faith with a clear conscience. See the commentary on 1 Tim 5:1-16 for an example of the church's creation of the role model of widow.

The Pastorals Have No Unified Model of Church Government

I repeat here an observation I have made time and again. The Pastorals draw their models of church leadership from different traditions and make little attempt to harmonize these models. For example, the author of the Pastorals is not interested in showing how deaconesses (1 Tim 3:11) function alongside of widows (1 Tim 5:3-16). Both "offices" can exist in one and the same church. He does not solve the problem of how the bishop was related to the elders (compare 1 Tim 3:1-7, 1 Tim 5:17-22, and Titus 1:5-9). When we look at our passage closely, we see that our author does not give us much of a clue as to how the deacon related to the bishop and vice versa. He seems to be saying to his churches: Consider these various ways of organizing the church. They have proved very useful in preserving, handing on, and developing the apostolic tradition; they have been effective in combatting heresy.

Some Perplexing Verses - Verses 2,6,11 and 12

Verses 2,6,11 and 12 have been the subject of discussion for decades. I will comment on them briefly.

Bishops and deacons are to be "husbands of one wife" (verses 2 and 12; see also Titus 1:6 and 1 Tim 5:9). What does the author mean by "husband of *one* wife"? I am becoming more convinced that the author refers to exemplary married life and not to the number of times a person has been married. In a society which, on the pagan side, knew of quick divorces and marriage-destroying liaisons and, on the Jewish side, of multiple successive marriages, the author holds up the ideal of faithful marriage.

Verse 6 comes from the church's experience of winning over converts of high standing in society. There would be great pressure exerted to install them as "bishops." The devil was God's high-ranking official, but pride seized his head. He fell, and was condemned. Let's not let what happened to the devil happen to our recent, high-ranking converts.

The final verse we scan is verse 11. The translation has: "The women likewise . . ." I have opted to translate the Greek word for "women" by "deaconesses." How do I justify my translation? First, the Greek word usually translated by "deacon" is a generic word and can mean either deacon or deaconess. Context decides whether a man or a woman is in mind; see Rom 16:1 where the woman's name Phoebe determines that the common Greek word *diakonos* be translated as "deaconess." So the author uses the word "women" in a context of exhortatory material on male church leaders to make it clear that he now has "deaconesses" in mind. Second, if the author intended verse 11 to deal with the wives of the deacons, he would have had to specify "women" with a possessive adjective like "*their* wives." Third, the word "likewise" used in verses 8 and 11 seems to be the author's way of introducing a new category of church leader. If so, then verse 11 would be dealing with the new category of deaconess. Fourth and finally, to insist that the author would never inset verse 11 about deaconesses into a unit which deals entirely with male deacons (verses 8-13) misunderstands exhortatory style, whose nature is to loosely connect different traditions.

The Permanent Value of This Passage

A judgment about the permanent value of this passage lies in our assessment of its adaptation of societal norms. To get us on that wavelength, let us move closer to home and look at a contemporary ecclesiastical norm for church leaders. In 1977 the United States Catholic Conference published the booklet, *As One Who Serves: Reflections on the Pastoral Ministry of Priests in the United States*. In it the authors adapted the contemporary "human growth" model as the background against which to view priestly ministers. Here are salient passages:

> The person who is a servant leader is expected to be a healthy, maturing person . . . . Priests are ordinary men, with the ordinary emotional, intellectual, and spiritual needs of normal people. Traditionally priests have been set apart, idealized, and treated as extraordinary, consecrated personages . . . . The social sciences have offered insights and analyses concerning behavioral dimensions which have come to be realized as common to all. As a human person, the priest desires to live on forever . . . Like any other human being, the priest wants to be accepted . . . Like others he searches for intimacy with his God, and struggles to integrate his life in the presence of the Lord (pp. 55-56).

It seems to me that norms for a church leader have not dropped from the heavens. Like the Pastorals, the United

States bishops have recognized the need for leaders in the church. Like the Pastorals, the United States bishops have looked to society for help in determining the qualities of these leaders. One of the best recommendations people can make about a candidate for church leadership is to say that that person is a fine human being. And in saying that, these people must needs draw upon what our society means by "a fine human being." And in doing that, they are doing what the churches of the Pastorals did as they assessed their candidates for positions of church leadership.

THE PAULINE, ECCLESIOLOGICAL, AND CHRISTOLOGICAL FOUNDATIONS OF CHURCH ORDER.
1 Tim 3:14-16.

> [14]I hope to come to you soon, but I am writing these instructions to you so that, [15]if I am delayed, you may know how one ought to behave in the household of God, which is the church of the living God, the pillar and bulwark of the truth. [16]Great indeed, we confess, is the mystery of our religion:
> He was manifested in the flesh,
> vindicated in the Spirit,
>   seen by angels,
> preached among the nations,
> believed on in the world,
>   taken up in glory.

These three verses are among the most important in all the Pastorals, for they give the Pauline, ecclesiological, and christological foundations of church order. I use three images to plumb the depths of this passage.

The Image of a Memorial
When I was in graduate school in Washington, D.C., I periodically toured the memorials dedicated to former presidents of the United States. Invariably these memorials

consisted of a statue or image of the president as well as a selection of his great sayings. These images and inscriptions tried to capture the vision and character of the leader and invited reflection on his meaning for today. This section is like those memorials. It presents the author's image of Paul, shares some of his most profound sayings on church and Christ Jesus, and invites our reflection on them. In the following paragraphs I accept that invitation and share my reflections with you.

The author of the Pastorals knows that Paul has been permanently delayed by martyrdom from ever meeting Timothy, but in the style of pseudonymous writing he portrays Paul as alive and giving "these instructions" (those of 2:1-3:13) for the church. The Apostle Paul does not leave his church in the lurch, but gives guidelines for its future.

The author dedicates verse 15 to his understanding of "the household of God, the church of the living God, the pillar and bulwark of the truth." These formulas are probably derived from the liturgy and need to be interpreted from the context of the Pastorals if we are to discern the author's understanding of them. Since the author uses "household" in 3:4,5,12 to refer to relationships between human beings, it is most probable that he means the same thing in this verse. To help us appreciate his thought more faithfully, I make two observations about "household." First, we should remember that "household" did not mean the same thing to him as it does to us. Most often we use the term in a very restricted sense: a household consists of parents and children. The author's understanding is the Greco-Roman one:

> In New Testament times the household was regarded as a basic political unity. In addition to members of the immediate family, slaves, freedmen, servants, laborers, and sometimes business associates and tenants were included . . . . The closeness of the household unit offered the security and sense of belonging not provided by larger political and social structures (A. J. Malherbe, *Social Aspects of Early Christianity*, p. 69).

So "household of God" conjures up the image of a group of people who are open-handed, welcoming, offering warmth and a sense of belonging. It is not a "closed" image. If that were the case, people like widows (1 Tim 5:3-16) would never be able to crack the inner circle.

My second point on "household" will help us better understand the many admonitions given different people in 1 Tim. A tradition going back to Aristotle and very much alive at the turn of the first Christian century has this to say about "household":

> And now that it is clear what are the component parts of the state, we have first of all to discuss household management; for every state is composed of households. Household management falls into departments corresponding to the parts of which the household in its turn is composed; and the household in its perfect form consists of slaves and freemen. The investigation of everything should begin with its smallest parts, and the primary and smallest parts of the household are master and slave, husband and wife, father and children; we ought therefore to examine the proper constitution and character of each of these three relationships, I mean that of mastership, that of marriage . . . and thirdly the progenitive relationship . . . . There is also a department which some people consider the same as household management and others the most important part of it, and the true position of which we shall have to consider: I mean what is called the art of getting wealth (Aristotle, *Politics* I, 1253, lines 1-14 in Loeb translation).

While "household of God" may conjure up, from one perspective, the image of a group of people who welcome outsiders, it also conjures up the image of order within the household. The image of "household of God" says that you are welcome to join the group, but we do have some regulations for the members of our household.

"The church of the living God" is interpreted best from 1 Tim 4:10, a passage within the immediate context of 3:15

and the only other passage in the Pastorals which has the phrase "the living God." 1 Tim 4:10 reads: "For to this end we toil and strive, because we have our hope set on the living God, who is the Savior of all men, especially of those who believe." The Christians assembled into the church set their hopes, not on a dead idol, but on a living God who directs them as he pursues his purpose of being the Savior of all people.

The secret or "mystery" which God has proclaimed in the ears of the Christians is the epitome of the truth of which the church is the pillar and bulwark. The christological hymn of verse 16 is arranged chronologically and antithetically. Chronologically seen, the lines refer to: 1) incarnation; 2) resurrection; 3) ascension; 4) the preaching of the gospel; 5) acceptance of the gospel in the world; 6) glorification at the end of time. Seen antithetically, the lines contain a contrast between earthly and other-earthly. Thus, if we identify earthly as A and other-earthly as B, the pattern of the hymn is: ABBAAB. The context of gnostic heresy (see the commentaries on 1 Tim 2:1-7, 8-15; 4:1-16) indicates that the author cites this hymn because it accentuates the earthly and universal dimensions of the Christ event: he was manifested *in the flesh*, preached *among the nations*, believed on *in the world*. And if there is to be universal preaching of the Christ event, there has to be some order in the church. Thus this hymn provides the christological basis for the instructions which order the church in 2:1-3:13. "Preached among the nations, believed on in the world" do not describe a fully accomplished fact for the church of the Pastorals. They set forth a goal for the church. It must not rest on its laurels, it must engage in mission to all. And it can do this with confidence in the living God, who wills the salvation of all (1 Tim 2:4).

In conclusion, the image of a memorial helps us to appreciate what the author is about in these three key verses. He undergirds the instructions of 2:1-3:13 by his understanding of Paul, Church, and Christ Jesus.

The Image of Summit

Verses 14-16 are like a summit. From their heights we can look backwards and forwards in 1 Tim. If we look backwards towards 2:1-3:13, we can appreciate the author's stress on order. "Quiet and peaceful lives," respect for the order of creation, leaders who lead irreproachable lives by society's and the church's standards, all these promote the mission of the church which is God's instrument for having the gospel "preached among the nations, believed on in the world." If we look back from this summit, we can appreciate the author's view of the church as a household which is made up of men and women and which has leaders who govern their own households well.

If we glance forwards to 4:1-6:21 from the summit of verses 14-16, especially from its vantage point of the church as "household," we notice further instructions for members of this household; Timothy, the model young church leader (4:1-16), widows (5:3-16), elders (5:17-22), slaves (6:1-2). There is also instruction on what to do about "making wealth" (6:5-10, 17-19). There are admonitions on how to cope with those who attack the truth (4:1-11; 6:3-10). There is concern about the missionary aspect of Christian conduct (5:14; 6:1). There is emphasis on the baptismal obligation of bearing witness before the world as Jesus did (6:11-16).

The Image of Vision

What vision of Paul, Church, and Christ Jesus does the author project in these verses? It is the image of a Paul who cares deeply for the church and leaves it the legacy of the instructions of 1 Tim 2:1-3:14. It is the vision of the church as a household, whose Master invites all to join his household. It is the vision of a church which wants to share its truth with all and engages in missionary activity to the nations. It is the vision of a church which is a bulwark against those who would eliminate the human and earthly dimensions of salvation. It is the vision of a church which realizes that it needs order if it is to be true to its call to preach the gospel in the world. And behind all these visions of the church stands the author's vision of God. God in Christ Jesus is in love with the world, with creation, with humankind. He wills the salvation of all. Because this is who its God is, the church has hope and engages in mission, a mission inspired by a Paul who knew first-hand that God is faithful to his promises (see 2 Tim).

DIFFERENT VISIONS OF REALITY.
1 Tim 4:1-16.

4 Now the Spirit expressly says that in later times some will depart from the faith by giving heed to deceitful spirits and doctrines of demons, ²through the pretensions of liars whose consciences are seared, ³who forbid marriage and enjoin abstinence from foods which God created to be received with thanksgiving by those who believe and know the truth. ⁴For everything created by God is good, and nothing is to be rejected if it is received with thanksgiving; ⁵for then it is consecrated by the word of God and prayer.

⁶If you put these instructions before the brethren, you will be a good minister of Christ Jesus, nourished on the words of the faith and of the good doctrine which you have followed. ⁷Have nothing to do with godless and silly myths. Train yourself in godliness; ⁸for while bodily training is of some value, godliness is of value in every way, as it holds promise for the present life and also for the life to come. ⁹The saying is sure and worthy of full acceptance. ¹⁰For to this end we toil and strive, because we have our hope set on the living God, who is the Savior of all men, especially of those who believe.

¹¹Command and teach these things. ¹²Let no one despise your youth, but set the believers an example in speech and conduct, in love, in faith, in purity. ¹³Till I come, attend to the public reading of scripture, to preaching, to teaching. ¹⁴Do not neglect the gift you have, which

was given you by prophetic utterance when the elders laid their hands upon you. [15]Practice these duties, devote yourself to them, so that all may see your progress. [16]Take heed to yourself and to your teaching: hold to that, for by so doing you will save both yourself and your hearers.

There is an old saw which can help us focus on the meaning of this section: "Two men looked out of the prison bars. One saw stars, the other saw mud." The vision these men had of life determined the way they saw reality. In this section the gnostic vision of reality is confronted with the Christian. The gnostic sees reality as evil; the Christian as good. The gnostics' view of reality determines that they will repudiate the institutions of society; the Christians' view determines that they will embrace them. In this section the Christian view of reality is couched in the literary form of exhortations to church leaders. See the imperatives in verses 6, 11, and 15. In our commentary we stop in three ports.

Connection with 1 Tim 3:14-16
This section flows easily from the all-important 1 Tim 3:14-16. It lays down regulations on how Christians should "behave in the household of God." Christians honor marriage and eat foods in thanksgiving. They pursue godliness. Young church leaders should be models for all. By its conduct and teaching the church should be a "pillar and bulwark of the truth" against the gnostics who deny the goodness of God's creation. "The mystery of our religion" teaches that humankind, world, and earth are good.

The Christian Views Creation and Institutions as Good
Since I have presented sufficient background on the gnostic character of the heresy in the commentaries on 1 Tim 2:1-15 and 2 Tim 2:14-3:9, it is not necessary to repeat that material here. It is important, however, to accentuate the author's theology of creation. Christians who know the truth (verse 3) realize that everything created by God is

good (verse 4). Their table prayers of thanksgiving, which contain words from scripture, teach them that creation is good (verses 4-5). Creation is not to be scorned as the work of some evil or inferior god. All are to be nourished on such words of faith, and are to follow faithfully the good doctrine that creation is good (verse 6).

Whereas in verses 3-6 the author argued against the gnostics' teaching on abstinence from foods, in verses 7-10 he argues not only against their views on abstinence but also against their views on the institution of marriage. His argumentation is in language which is not immediately understandable to us: "Train yourself in godliness" (verse 7). What does he mean by "godliness"? "To act godly" means to perform one's duties, e.g., caring for one's parents. See 1 Tim 5:4: "If a widow has children or grandchildren, let them first learn their religious duty to their own family . . . ." I find a contemporary example of what "godliness" means in the campaign literature I receive at election time. The man running for political office is described as a regular church-goer, a hometown boy, a family man, one who cares for his elderly parents, one who has served in the armed forces, one who is active in a host of civic and charitable organizations. Much of what the author means by "godliness" is captured in the qualifications this candidate boasts. To lack them is to be ungodly, that is, to be an atheist, to be against country, to be against the welfare of one's fellow human beings. The author says that the gnostics' pursuit of the bodily disciplines of abstinence from sex and food may temporarily impress people, but that in the long run people will realize their transitory character. The pursuit of godliness is of absolute value and promises life in the present and in the future (verse 8). This teaching on godliness is so important that it is a "sure saying" (verse 9). It is so important that it is worth the pain and suffering of striving for its implementation (verse 10).

In the commentary on 1 Tim 2:1-7 I addressed myself to the question of the "bourgeois" or middle-class ethic of the Pastorals. In verses 7-10 we encounter another aspect of this ethic. The author does not stress the church's need

for institutions and structures merely because the church
has evolved so far that it needs them lest chaos set in. The
author does not stress structure in the church merely because through such structures the church can more effectively combat heresy. The author stresses structure in the
church and enjoins respect for the structures of society
because of his vision of reality. Creation and human institutions are not to be repudiated as the gnostics do. "Train
yourself in godliness" promotes a vision of reality. This
vision of reality also explains why the author frequently
insists on conduct which is irreproachable according to
society's norms. See 1 Tim 6:1: "Let all who are under the
yoke of slavery regard their masters as worthy of all honor,
*so that the name of God and the teaching may not be
defamed.*" Of course, with our more sophisticated views
of society we can sit back and take the author of the Pastorals to task because he did not know about institutional
evil or evil social structures. His views would lead to promo-
tion of such evil social structures. But to criticize the author
on that account would be anachronistic. Seen from the
perspective of his day and situation, he affirms realities
which the gnostics were denying. God the creator is involved
in the everyday. Salvation is not to be found in some im-
pressive ascetic practices, but in the pursuit of godliness
which upholds those institutions which benefit humankind.
It is provocative to compare the conclusion of verse 8 with
the gospel saying upon which it is based: "Truly, I say to
you, there is no man who has left house or wife or brothers
or parents or children, for the sake of the kingdom of God,
who will not receive manifold more in this time, and in the
age to come eternal life" (Lk 18:29-30). For the author of
the Pastorals, full-bodied involvement in the things of
creation promises life in the present and in the future.

Church Leaders Promote the Christian Vision of Reality

Five points call for comment in this part. First, church
leaders like Timothy are to teach the Christian vision of
reality. Both leaders and people are to be nourished on such

words of the faith and are to live lives in accordance with the faith.

Second, through the person of Timothy the author asks his communities to consider young men for leadership posts. (See the parallel passage in Titus 2:6-7.) By "young man" the author probably means someone between thirty and forty years of age. Verse 14 points out the innovative character of this lowering of the age requirement for a church leader, especially if we follow another possible way of translating that verse, namely, "when hands were laid upon you to make you an elder." An "elder" is no longer the leader who is elder in age; an "elder" can be a young man.

Third, it is not clear who lays on hands for ordination. In point number two above we saw the different ways of viewing the laying on of hands described in verse 14. 1 Tim 5:22 refers to Timothy as the one who lays on hands. In 2 Tim 1:6 the Apostle Paul lays on hands. Rather than try to harmonize these different passages, I suggest that we view them as a further example of the fluidity of church structure promoted by the author of the Pastorals. There is to be ordination through the laying on of hands, but it is not rigidly determined who it is who lays on hands.

Fourth, 1 Tim 1:18 reads: "This charge I commit to you, Timothy, my son, in accordance with the *prophetic utterances* which pointed to you." Verse 14 in this section reads: "Which was given you by *prophetic utterance.*" In the fluid stage of church structure described in the Pastorals it seems that prophets in the community singled out a person for a position of church leadership. The best parallel for this phenomenon is found in Acts 13:1-3: "Now in the church at Antioch there were prophets and teachers . . . . While they were worshipping the Lord and fasting, the Holy Spirit said, 'Set apart for me Barnabas and Saul for the work to which I have called them.' Then after fasting and praying they laid their hands on them and sent them off." The Holy Spirit chose Barnabas and Saul through the utterances of Christian prophets.

Fifth, in verse 14 the author uses the word "gift" (*charisma* in Greek; recall our English expression, "He's got charisma!"). He uses the same word in 2 Tim 1:6: "Hence I remind you to rekindle the *gift* of God that is within you through the laying on of my hands." Charisma/gift is a Pauline term. See 1 Cor 12-14 where Paul treats of the various gifts of the Spirit. Our author hands on this aspect of the Pauline deposit. But since his main concern is with leaders in the church, he does not discuss charisms in general nor the role which the individual charisms like prophecy play in the church. His chief concern is that Timothy use his charism: he should not neglect it, he should rekindle it. On the one hand, the author has been faithful to the Pauline deposit by preserving the Pauline notion that God's gifts enable service in the church. On the other hand, he has gone beyond that deposit by stressing the permanence of the charisma/gift; it can be rekindled and neglected. The charisma/gift involves certain responsibilities and duties like the public reading of scripture, preaching, and teaching (verse 13).

In sum, Christians and their leaders are to strive to view reality as God's good creation. They are to put their faith into practice by respecting the institutions and structures which society has created to promote human welfare. The church leaders, gifted by God for service to the church, should be an example of virtue to the rest of the flock.

FUNDAMENTAL CHRISTIAN VALUES.
1 Tim 5:1-16.

5 Do not rebuke an older man but exhort him as you would a father; treat younger men like brothers, ²older women like mothers, younger women like sisters, in all purity.

³Honor widows who are real widows. ⁴If a widow has children or grandchildren, let them first learn their religious duty to their own family and make some return

to their parents; for this is acceptable in the sight of God. [5]She who is a real widow, and is left all alone, has set her hope on God and continues in supplications and prayers night and day; [6]whereas she who is self-indulgent is dead even while she lives. [7]Command this, so that they may be without reproach. [8]If any one does not provide for his relatives, and especially for his own family, he has disowned the faith and is worse than an unbeliever.

[9]Let a widow be enrolled if she is not less than sixty years of age, having been the wife of one husband; [10]and she must be well attested for her good deeds, as one who has brought up children, shown hospitality, washed the feet of the saints, relieved the afflicted, and devoted herself to doing good in every way. [11]But refuse to enrol younger widows; for when they grow wanton against Christ they desire to marry, [12]and so they incur condemnation for having violated their first pledge. [13]Besides that, they learn to be idlers, gadding about from house to house, and not only idlers but gossips and busybodies, saying what they should not. [14]So I would have younger widows marry, bear children, rule their households, and give the enemy no occasion to revile us. [15]For some have already strayed after Satan. [16]If any believing woman has relatives who are widows, let her assist them; let the church not be burdened, so that it may assist those who are real widows.

In this section the author continues to detail regulations for conduct "in the household of God" (1 Tim 3:15). The rules in verses 1-2 have deep roots in Greek society. The regulations in verses 3-16 are Christian creations. I group my remarks in this section around verses 1-2 and 3-16.

The Traditional Norms of Verses 1-2

By now we have come to expect that the author of the Pastorals will not place all his regulations for a church leader in one place. In this section he adapts norms from yet another Greco-Roman hortatory tradition. As early as Plato, this ideal of conduct was inculcated: "For no matter whom he meets, he will feel that he is meeting a brother, a sister, a father, a mother, a son, a daughter" (Plato, *Republic* 5.463c, Loeb translation). Many a honorific inscription praised a man for such conduct. A first century B.C. inscription reads: "Continually honoring older men as parents, peers as brothers, and younger men as sons" (translation from M. Dibelius; H. Conzelmann, *The Pastoral Epistles*, p. 72). The church leader's power should not go to his head. In accordance with the finest Greco-Roman tradition, he should respect those he "rebukes."

The Creative Norms of Verses 3-16

In the commentary on verses 1-2 above and in the commentaries on previous sections of 1 Tim I have called your attention to the author's penchant for adapting norms from his contemporary Greco-Roman society. In verses 3-16 we have a unique opportunity to see the author's creativity. Since he found no acceptable Greco-Roman societal norms with regard to the care of totally abandoned widows, the author had to create norms for the widows in his communities. We look at his creative work from many angles in the following paragraphs.

A. Conflicting Traditions on Care of Widows

All of us are acquainted with the plight of the widow in contemporary society, but that plight in no way compares with that of the widow in antiquity. The widow in Greco-Roman tradition was trapped in a patriarchal system. Once her protector and "breadwinner" died, she was cast adrift. There was no welfare system, no social security to come to her rescue. There is a strong clash between this tradition and the Judeo-Christian tradition which insisted that widows be cared for. We read in Dt 27:19: "'Cursed be he who perverts the justice due to the sojourner, the fatherless, and the widow.'" The prophets railed against those who abused the widow: "Father and mother are treated with contempt in you; the sojourner suffers extortion in your midst; the fatherless and the widow are wronged in you" (Ezek 22:7). If the author had remained locked within his Greco-Roman tradition which did not teach care for widows in distress, he would never have recognized their situation as a plight, let alone given regulations to his church for their care.

In the above paragraph I have telescoped much. Perhaps a contemporary analogy will help us appreciate some of what is going on between the lines of verses 3-16. In a country where apartheid is law, there is a traditional white household. As the members of that household reflect upon the implications of their Christian faith, they decide to go against the law of the land and to take an "outcast" into their household as a full member. Behind the scenes of verses 3-16 there is soul-searching similar to that which pulsed through the members of that Christian white household before they accepted an "outcast" as a full member of their heart and hearth.

B. The Importance of Women in the Church

The importance of the order of widow should not be viewed from our contemporary perspective which frequently places bishops and priests on a pedestal, but from the perspective of that time. Ponder the innovative and courageous faith which led the author to enrol women as office-holders within a patriarchal "household of God."

C. Who is a "Real Widow"?

In verses 3-16 the author is creatively working towards a definition of a "real widow." The untidiness of verses 3-16 reveals a genius at work. Allow me to assemble the pieces he has scattered about in these verses:

> A real widow (verses 3,5,16) is at least sixty years old (verse 9). She has been married just once (verse 9). She has distinguished herself within the community by

numerous acts of charity (verse 10). She prays day and
night, having set her hope on God alone (verse 5). She is
financially supported by the community (verse 16). She is
formally enrolled into the order of widows (verse 9) and
commits herself to it permanently (verse 12). Seen negatively, widows who are not all alone (verse 5), widows
who have families who can support them (verses 4,8), and
widows who are supported by a "believing woman"
(verse 16) are not to be considered "real widows."

D. What Did a "Real Widow" Do?

First, a real widow is absorbed in God and prayer (verse
5). At first blush, this seems to be yet another instance of
the author's insistence on the need for prayer. Further
reflection, however, carries us deeper into the author's
meaning. If we recall that in the Old Testament the widow
was a symbol of total dependence upon God, then we
begin to see another element in her "job description." By
her life of prayer and total dedication to God a real widow
summons the Christian community to examine its stance
towards the world. Yes, creation is good, and Christians
should frolic in it. It is not evil as the gnostics claim. But
while creation contains the footprints of God, it is not God.
To be totally absorbed in the world and to seek pleasure
as the sum and substance of life lead to death. True life is
found in God alone (verse 7). The widow, then, is a symbol
of transcendence in a world-affirming community.

Commentators are divided on whether verses 10 and 13
point to the real widow's other responsibilities within the
community. My position is that they do. Even though
verse 10 is taken up with the widow's past record of Christian service, there seems to be no reason to restrict her
performance of these good deeds to the past. Even though
age (in antiquity sixty was a "good" age) may have reduced
her strength, she continues her charitable activities (verse
10) and her pastoral visits (verse 13). These are her
responsibilities.

E. The Author At His Creative Best

First, let's look at verses 4 and 8 which are very similar to one another, and, along with verse 16, are formulated in the "if" or conditional style. Allow me to quote verses 4 and 8 in full:

> If a widow has children or grandchildren, let them first learn their religious duty to their own family and make some return to their parents; *for this is acceptable in the sight of God* (verse 4).

> If any one does not provide for his relatives, and especially for his own family, *he has disowned the faith* and is worse than an unbeliever (verse 8).

In 1 Tim 2:3, on the basis of a creed which professed God as savior of all, the author argued that prayer for all people was "acceptable in the sight of God our Savior." In 1 Tim 5:4 the author maintains that care for one's widowed parent is acceptable in the sight of God. He bases his case on the law of care of parents, upheld by both Jews and pagans. In verse 8 he states his case much more forcefully. Failure to care for widowed parents is equivalent to disowning the faith. This is such a powerful statement that we should pause and reflect on it further. What does the author mean by "the faith"? How can neglect of a social obligation be equated with the abandonment of one's faith? If we grant the author's teaching throughout these pastoral epistles that faith must issue in good deeds, then we can begin to glimpse his meaning here. By "the faith" he means acceptance of societal and Old Testament norms of what a good deed is. To go against these norms is to deny the faith. By drawing upon these norms, the author creatively handles one aspect of the problem of the plight of widows within his communities.

Second, in verses 7, 10, and 14 the author draws upon another of his creations, the principle of "irreproachable conduct." (That principle is also at work in 1 Tim 3:2,7,10; 6:1; Titus 1:6,7; 2:5,8,10.) We begin with verse 10, where the author states the principle of "irreproachable conduct" positively - "well attested." In dealing with widows, the church had virtually no precedents in Jewish or Greco-Roman society for what "good behavior" for widows is. It is behavior filled with the doing of "good deeds." (The specification of these "good deeds" in verse 10 gives us a good idea of what to read into other passages in the Pastorals where the author simply mentions "good deeds"; see 1 Tim 2:10; 6:18; 2 Tim 2:21; 3:17; Titus 1:16; 2:7,14: 3:1, 8,14.) A Christian good deed is to bring up orphans ("brought up children"), to show hospitality, to wash the feet of the saints (in imitation of Jesus; see Jn 13:1-20), to relieve the afflicted. In 1 Tim 3:1-7 the author drew upon Greco-Roman societal norms for his description of the qualifications of a bishop. Here he is at his creative best in setting forth Christian norms. The widow who has performed these acts of charity would surely have manifested "irreproachable conduct" within the community. (As a matter of fact, these acts of social concern would establish any Christian's good reputation within the community, for none of these deeds is the exclusive domain of a widow.)

Commentators regularly interpret verse 7 as a reference to widows: "Command this, so that they may be *without reproach.*" But it seems more in accord with the author's exhortatory style to interpret "this" (the Greek has "these") as a reference to the content of verses 3-6. The author wants the conduct of the widow's children and grandchildren to be irreproachable (see verse 4). If these neglected their widowed mother and grandmother, they would offend against pagan societal norms and bring reproach upon the Christian community.

In verse 14 the author is again concerned with the reputation of Christians among non-Christians. The non-Christian community might be puzzled by the behavior of the "real widows," but would not find fault with it. But the existence and activities of younger widows in the household of God might easily supply non-Christian scandal-mongers with plenty of ammunition (see verse 13). So the author places the strong directive of verse 14 in Paul's mouth. Younger widows should follow the societal norms for women their age; they will find salvation in marriage (see 1 Tim 2:15). And the Christian reputation will be preserved.

F. Conclusion

In our discussion of verses 3-16 we have made a long journey. Let's glance back at the places we have stopped. In accordance with its Judeo-Christian heritage the community of the Pastorals cared for widows in distress. These widows, totally dedicated to God, were symbols of the Christians' utter dependence on God. These widows, cared for by the church, cared, in turn, for the members of the church. With the passage of time and the emergence of problems, the church began to establish clearer guidelines for widows.

In addressing himself to the "widow question," the author is creative and shows how he thinks when there are few Greco-Roman norms to rely on. The harvest of his thinking includes these points: 1) Christians are to authenticate their faith by action, especially by the good deeds of kindness to the needy; 2) they are to be open to God through prayer and not to get so immersed in affirming this world that they forget that their source of life is God; 3) what society prescribes as normative behavior is a vitally important guide for determining Christian conduct and faith; 4) the way to salvation is multi-avenued; the way of the "real widow" is a fine road, but there are others available to people like the younger widows; 5) women are as worthy as men of occupying positions of authority within the Christian community.

QUALITIES EXPECTED OF ELDERS.
1 Tim 5:17-25.

> [17]Let the elders who rule well be considered worthy of double honor, especially those who labor in preaching and teaching; [18]for the scripture says, "You shall not

muzzle an ox when it is treading out the grain," and, "The laborer deserves his wages." 19Never admit any charge against an elder except on the evidence of two or three witnesses. 20As for those who persist in sin, rebuke them in the presence of all, so that the rest may stand in fear. 21In the presence of God and of Christ Jesus and of the elect angels I charge you to keep these rules without favor, doing nothing from partiality. 22Do not be hasty in the laying on of hands, nor participate in another man's sins; keep yourself pure.

23No longer drink only water, but use a little wine for the sake of your stomach and your frequent ailments.

24The sins of some men are conspicuous, pointing to judgment, but the sins of others appear later. 25So also good deeds are conspicuous; and even when they are not, they cannot remain hidden.

In this section the author of the Pastorals presents still another type of church government to the communities which fly the flag of Paul. In this type, a college or board of elders is at the helm. We make three observations on this passage.

Connection with the Preceding Verses

This section is connected to its immediate context by the concepts of honor and financial support. The author began his instructions about widows with the imperative "honor" (1 Tim 5:3) and concluded them with a reference to the financial assistance which the community gives to "real widows" (verse 16). He begins this section by discussing the financial remuneration to be given those elders within the college who do their tasks well (verses 17-18). They are to be given "double honor," that is, a double honorarium. In the broader context of the epistle this section relates back to the cardinal passage of 1 Tim 3:14-16 and treats of the role of elders in "the household of God."

Elders Who Lead Irreproachable Lives and Preach and Teach

In the commentary on 1 Tim we have repeatedly noticed that the author does not champion one style of church structure. He insists that there should be structure to ensure the faithful transmission and development of the Pauline deposit of faith. But he leaves it to individual communities to adapt those structures they deem fit, provided that the leaders within these structures teach the gospel faithfully and lead irreproachable lives. This passage is in complete accord with the author's intention. A community may be governed by a college of elders as long as the elders faithfully preach and teach the gospel and repulse opponents (verse 17; see also 1 Tim 3:2 and Titus 1:9), and as long as careful steps are taken to select elders of the highest moral qualifications (verses 22,24-25). Timothy and those like him should not be hasty to ordain someone as an elder (verse 22). They should engage in considerable discernment to make sure that only those distinguished by "good deeds" are selected as elders (verse 25).

In sum, the author, while stressing the need for structure, allows for various styles of church government, one of which is a college of elders. He commands that within these various structures the gospel is faithfully preached by leaders whose conduct is blameless.

The Unity of the Theme Within the Passage

In the preceding section of commentary I presupposed that this passage deals with one theme, and one theme only, that of the church structure of elders. Some commentators hold a different view. According to them, in verse 20 the author moves away from the theme of elders and begins to discuss the Christian life in general. The highpoint of their interpretation is that verse 22 does not refer to the laying-on-of-hands performed in ordination, but to the laying-on-of-hands performed in the reconciliation of sinners. How do I protect my flanks against this alternate interpretation? (Verse 23 is a digression which gives evidence of the practical spirituality of the author.)

In the commentaries on 1 Tim 1:3-20 and 2 Tim 2:14-26 I
provide full-scale models of how the author argues. Here
space-limits command brevity. The author argues, in the
style of exhortation, by means of catchwords. Connexions
between verses 17-20 are made by the catchword of the
"who" clauses which modify "elder"; "elders *who rule well*"
(verse 17); "those elders *who labor* in preaching and teaching" (verse 17); "as for those *who persist* in sin" (verse 20).
Verse 20 concludes the author's use of that catchword and
initiates a new one, "sin," which continues his train of
thought about "elder" and moves it to a new level: "as for
those who persist in *sin*" (verse 20); "nor participate in
another man's *sins*" (verse 22); "the *sins* of some men are
conspicuous" (verse 24). Thus, the author moves from positive admonitions about elders (verses 17-18) to negative
ones (verses 19-22,24), and concludes with a positive one
(verse 25).

In conclusion, in verse 22 the author does not depart from
his characteristic themes to teach a quick one-liner about
reconciliation of sinners. In his desire to provide leaders
of impeccable moral quality for the churches, the author
exhorts Timothy and those like him to use utmost care in
the selection of those they will ordain elders.

LIFE AND THE HOUSEHOLD OF GOD.
1 Tim 6:1-21.

> **6** Let all who are under the yoke of slavery regard
> their masters as worthy of all honor, so that the name
> of God and the teaching may not be defamed. ²Those
> who have believing masters must not be disrespectful
> on the ground that they are brethren; rather they must
> serve all the better since those who benefit by their
> service are believers and beloved.
>
> Teach and urge these duties. ³If any one teaches other-
> wise and does not agree with the sound words of our
> Lord Jesus Christ and the teaching which accords with
> godliness, ⁴he is puffed up with conceit, he knows nothing;
> he has a morbid craving for controversy and for disputes
> about words, which produce envy, dissension, slander,

base suspicions, [5]and wrangling among men who are depraved in mind and bereft of the truth, imagining that godliness is a means of gain. [6]There is great gain in godliness with contentment; [7]for we brought nothing into the world, and we cannot take anything out of the world; [8]but if we have food and clothing, with these we shall be content. [9]But those who desire to be rich fall into temptation, into a snare, into many senseless and hurtful desires that plunge men into ruin and destruction. [10]For the love of money is the root of all evils; it is through this craving that some have wandered away from the faith and pierced their hearts with many pangs.

[11]But as for you, man of God, shun all this; aim at righteousness, godliness, faith, love, steadfastness, gentleness. [12]Fight the good fight of the faith; take hold of the eternal life to which you were called when you made the good confession in the presence of many witnesses. [13]In the presence of God who gives life to all things, and of Christ Jesus who in his testimony before Pontius Pilate made the good confession, [14]I charge you to keep the commandment unstained and free from reproach until the appearing of our Lord Jesus Christ; [15]and this will be made manifest at the proper time by the blessed and only Sovereign, the King of kings and Lord of lords, [16]who alone has immortality and dwells in unapproachable light, whom no man has ever seen or can see. To him be honor and eternal dominion. Amen.

[17]As for the rich in this world, charge them not to be haughty, nor to set their hopes on uncertain riches but on God who richly furnishes us with everything to enjoy. [18]They are to do good, to be rich in good deeds, liberal and generous, [19]thus laying up for themselves a good foundation for the future, so that they may take hold of the life which is life indeed.

[20]O Timothy, guard what has been entrusted to you. Avoid the godless chatter and contradictions of what is falsely called knowledge, [21]for by professing it some have missed the mark as regards the faith.

Grace be with you.

For some ten years now I have been pondering the meaning and structure of this passage. At times I think it is very orderly. At other times I think it is utter chaos. Why such vacillation? One of the reasons is the search for the connections between verses 11-16 which discuss baptism and verses 6-10 and 17-19 which discuss wealth. The other day it dawned on me that I was trying to find order where the author may have something else in mind. He is writing exhortation which is subject to rules different from those which order the writing of an orderly scholar. Having abandoned my image of an author athirst for order, I have hit upon a new one, that of an artist. This passage is like an unfinished painting. There is enough shape in the painting for viewers to spot the artist's intention, but enough unfinished areas for viewers to use their own creative imaginations to complete the painting. I title the author's unfinished painting "Life and the Household of God." In the following paragraphs I will highlight the general structure and shapes of the author's unfinished painting.

The General Structure of the Passage

This section concludes the author's treatment of "how one ought to behave in the household of God" (1 Tim 3:15). As we saw in the commentary on 1 Tim 3:14-16, discussions of "household" dealt with the master's relationship to wife, children, slaves, and with the making of wealth. Having adapted the household model for many of the exhortations in this epistle, the author briefly treats of conduct expected of Christian slaves in verses 1-2. In verses 6-10 and 17-19 he employs two different traditions to discuss the making of wealth. Employing his best exhortatory style, the author connects his thoughts on conduct in the household to other key ideas by means of catchwords. The two main catchwords in this section are "godliness" and "life."

Before outlining this section to underscore the author's use of catchwords, I would like to quote from an earlier passage in 1 Tim where "godliness" and "life" were intimately linked: "*Godliness* is of value in every way, as it holds promise *for the present life* and also *for the life to*

come" (4:8). Echoes of this verse sound throughout 1 Tim
6:1-21, whose outline is:

6:1-2	-	exhortation to Christian slaves
6:3	-	"teaching which accords with *godliness*"
6:4-5a	-	stereotyped polemic vs. opponents
6:5b	-	"imagining that *godliness* is a means of gain."
6:6	-	"There is great gain in *godliness with* contentment."
6:11	-	"Shun all this; aim at righteousness, *godliness . . .*"
6:12	-	"Take hold of the *eternal life* to which you were called." (Here and in 1 Tim 4:8 we have the only two clear instances in which the author refers to "life" as a present possession.)
6:13	-	"In the presence of God *who gives life* to all things"
6:19	-	"So that they may take hold *of the life which is life indeed.*" (In the Pastorals the verb "to take hold of" is used only twice, in verses 12 and 19; by means of this catchword the author joins the diverse traditions of verses 12-16 and 17-19.)

In a word, then, the author concludes his epistle by
commenting on two final aspects of household management: slaves and making of wealth. He weaves these remarks together by means of the two threads of "godliness"
and "life." Now that we have detected the overall structure
of the unfinished painting of this section, let us take a
closer look at some of its key shapes or ideas.

The Key Ideas of This Passage

A. Godliness and the Things of This World

In the commentary on 1 Tim 4:1-16 I devoted considerable space to what the author means by "godliness." Here I
can only share highlights. "Godliness" means involvement
in those structures and institutions of society which promote
religion and human welfare. The "godly" person is the one

who goes to church, who has served country in military service, who is dedicated to spouse and family, who is active in civic organizations which foster the fine arts, etc. In the author's frame of reference "ungodly" persons are the gnostics who deny the goodness of creation and human institutions. In this section the author addresses himself to a further aspect of what is involved in "godliness," of what is involved in a theology which affirms creation: How should Christians monitor their immersion in the world? That the author gives two different answers to this question should not surprise us. Recall how many different models our flexible author has of church government, e.g., bishop, deaconesses, widows.

His first answer is modeled on Cynic-Stoic tradition: "There is great gain in godliness with contentment" (verse 6). The best general parallel to this verse and verses 7-10 is found in Diogenes Laertius' account of the Cynics:

> They also hold that we should live frugally, eating food for nourishment only and wearing a single garment. Wealth and fame and high birth they despise. Some at all events are vegetarians and drink cold water only and are content with any kind of shelter or tubs, like Diogenes, who used to say that it was the privilege of gods to need nothing and god-like men to want but little (*Lives of the Eminent Philosophers* 6.104; Loeb translation).

In brief, the author says that "godliness" or affirmation of the world does not mean that true life is to be found in "the desire to be rich" or "in the love of money," for these lead to "ruin and destruction," loss of faith, and many pangs of heart (verses 7-10). The author moderates the implications of his creation theology by means of the wisdom drawn from the Cynic-Stoic philosophical tradition.

The author's second answer in verses 17-19 is based on gospel tradition, e.g., Lk 12:21: "So is he who lays up treasure for himself, and is not rich towards God" (see also Lk 16:9 and Mt 6:20). The author's creation theology will not allow him to condemn the good things of life, for they come from "God who richly furnishes us with everything to enjoy" (verse 17). But Christians are not to use their possessions as a means of exalting themselves above God and their fellow human beings (verse 17). These possessions are to be used for others (verse 18). Without the good deeds of caring for others, there will not be life "which is life indeed" (verse 19).

As we look back over the author's two answers to the huge question of how to reconcile a creation theology with the "lure of the world," we may have more questions than answers. That's well and good. We can complete his unfinished painting. The author did the best he could, faced, as he was, with a world-hating gnostic heresy and situated in a culture which praised "godliness" and applauded a household in which "the making of wealth" was handled adroitly.

B. Life and Baptism

We saw in the preceding paragraphs that godliness is intimately related to life. In verses 12-16 the author adapts a baptismal tradition and gives us an even richer view of what he means by "life." (I do not agree with those commentators who interpret verses 12-16 as an ordination exhortation to church leaders.) The gift of eternal life now in baptism comes from a God who has already shown himself to be for life (verse 13). The experience of the Christian who at baptism made *the good confession* is paralleled to that of Christ Jesus who also made *the good confession* (verse 13). What is the meaning of this parallel? It is multidimensional. First, Christ Jesus was faithful to his call even though he had to undergo persecution because of that fidelity; during persecution Christians should be steadfast and faithful to God's call. Second, Christ Jesus' true existence in the flesh issued in his suffering at the time of Pontius Pilate; Christians should not try to flee their human existence, but make the good confession to God who called them as full human persons. Finally, Christ Jesus made the good confession which was in accord with a true understanding of who God is; Christians must make their good confession in accordance with "the sound words of our Lord Jesus Christ" (verse 3).

Christian life is initiated at baptism and lived after the model of the very human Christ Jesus (see 1 Tim 2:5). And while living life in expectation of "the appearing of our Lord Jesus Christ," Christians should "keep the commandment unstained and free from reproach" (verse 14). By "the commandment" the author means the pursuit of "godliness," the affirmation of the world, adherence to the sound teaching, and fidelity to the humanity of the Savior Christ Jesus during persecution. "The commandment" is like our present-day vows or promises.

In resume, at the end of his letter the author returns to the theme of "life," which he had hinted at earlier, and exhorts us to take its human and Christian dimensions seriously. As the plural "you" of his final words in verse 21 - "Grace be with *you*" - indicates, his message is for all. All of us are to complete the unfinished painting of "Life and the Household of God" by the witness of our lives in a pluralistic world.

C. Guard What Has Been Entrusted To You

The author concludes his letter in verses 20-21 with words that summarize many of his concerns. In the commentary on 2 Tim 1:6-14 I provide a full treatment of what is involved in "guarding the deposit." It is a creative process likened to the sharing of friends; it is not the inflexible handing on of some fixed entity from generation to generation. I conclude this part with an anecdote which would have gotten a chuckle out of the adventuresome author of the Pastorals. J. L. Houlden, former Principal of Cuddesdon Theological College, writes:

> And it is no accident that when ideals of priestly life and a sense of Church authority were revived in the Church of England in the nineteenth century, people

appealed constantly to these writings (the Pastorals). Cuddesdon Theological College, founded in devotion to these ideals in 1854, took I Tim 6:21 ('Guard the deposit') as its motto, inscribing it even upon its chamber-pots! (*The Pastoral Epistles*, pp. 15-16).

Conclusion

We have come to the conclusion of 1 Tim. And as I sit at my typewriter conjuring up an image of what it was all about, I am reminded of a poster some very dear friends of mine have in their study. It reads:

There are two lasting bequests
We can give our children -
One is roots,
The other, wings.

For a church in transition the author of the Pastorals has provided the roots of Paul's example (2 Tim) and his instructions on church structure and life (1 Tim), the roots of traditional understandings of the church (1 Tim 3:15), the roots of traditional creeds about Jesus (esp. 1 Tim 3:16), and the roots of baptismal tradition (1 Tim 6:12-16). A church in transition can be firmly grounded in these roots. The author also provides wings, so that in imitation of him the church can move into new times, countries, situations and adapt itself to them. And upon this process of rooting and winging there are the blessings of a very benevolent God and a very human Christ Jesus.

CHRISTIANS AFFIRM CREATION AND
HOPE IN GOD
Titus 1:1-4.

> **1** Paul, a servant of God and an apostle of Jesus Christ,
> to further the faith of God's elect and their knowledge of
> the truth which accords with godliness, ²in hope of
> eternal life which God, who never lies, promised ages
> ago ³and at the proper time manifested in his word
> through the preaching with which I have been entrusted
> by command of God our Savior;
> ⁴To Titus, my true child in a common faith:
> Grace and peace from God the Father and Christ
> Jesus our Savior.

If you are like me, you have received a letter from a friend
which contained sentences whose exact meaning eluded
you. You pondered them over and over again. These four
introductory verses are like those sentences you puzzled
over. Read through these verses slowly and often, noting
key words and phrases. In what follows I share with you the
results of my brooding over these verses.

Paul's Authority Stands Behind This Letter

One would hardly have expected the historical Paul to
write such a formal introduction to a close friend and
intimate associate as Titus. The formality of verses 1-4
indicates that the author envisions entire churches as his
audience. In these verses he leaves no doubt that the authority of Paul, *the* Apostle, stands behind the letter's contents.
This letter conveys Paul's preaching which manifests the
meaning of Christian life (verse 3).

In many respects, these four verses are an advance summary of the letter. In accordance with Paul's responsibility
of furthering "the knowledge of the truth" (verse 1) the
author presents Paul as giving directions on how to combat
those who oppose the truth (1:5-16) and as handing on
creedal summaries of that truth (2:11-15; 3:4-7). In 2:1-10

the author presents detailed instructions about conduct which is in accord with "godliness." Finally, in 2:13 and 3:7 he develops a bit further what he means by "in hope of eternal life" (verse 2).

Affirmation of the World and Hope in God

In my commentary on 1 Tim, the author's companion piece to Titus, I often noticed his world-affirming attitude. In the commentary on 1 Tim 6:1-21 I garnered those observations together and explored the author's way of reconciling his world-affirming attitudes with his hope in eternal life. Verses 1-3, which mention Paul's preaching, hope of eternal life, and a world-affirming attitude under the rubric of "godliness," afford me the opportunity of summarizing my reflections on these themes from 1 Tim and of carrying them a step deeper.

As the author writes this third exhortatory letter to Pauline communities, he operates with four principles. First, against his gnostic opponents he insists that God's creation is good and is to be used with thanksgiving. Second, while affirming the goodness of creation and of human institutions, the author does not equate "life" with life in this world. Third, Paul's preaching manifests and effects Christian life in this world. Christians will find true life in this world by adhering to Paul's preaching (verse 3). Fourth and finally, Christians, while affirming the world and while enjoying eternal life in the present, yearn for God and longingly await the appearance of Christ Jesus, their hope (verse 2). In the course of the commentary on the rest of Titus we will have occasion to see how the author runs with each of these four principles.

To recapitulate, the opening four verses of Titus are compact. If we spend time pondering their significance, we will be rewarded with avenues of approach to the rest of the letter and with insights into what the author means by life, hope, and the world.

THE MARKS OF A CHURCH IN TRANSITION.
Titus 1:5-16.

> [5]This is why I left you in Crete, that you might amend what was defective, and appoint elders in every town as I directed you, [6]if any man is blameless, the husband of one wife, and his children are believers and not open to the charge of being profligate or insubordinate. [7]For a bishop, as God's steward, must be blameless; he must not be arrogant or violent or greedy for gain, [8]but hospitable, a lover of goodness, master of himself, upright, holy, and self-controlled; [9]he must hold firm to the sure word as taught, so that he may be able to give instruction in sound doctrine and also to confute those who contradict it. [10]For there are many insubordinate men, empty talkers and deceivers, especially the circumcision party; [11]they must be silenced, since they are upsetting whole families by teaching for base gain what they have no right to teach. [12]One of themselves, a prophet of their own, said, "Cretans are always liars, evil beasts, lazy gluttons." [13]This testimony is true. Therefore rebuke them sharply, that they may be sound in the faith, [14]instead of giving heed to Jewish myths or to commands of men who reject the truth. [15]To the pure all things are pure, but to the corrupt and unbelieving nothing is pure; their very minds and consciences are corrupted. [16]They profess to know God, but they deny him by their deeds; they are detestable, disobedient, unfit for any good deed.

Some time ago I went to an art musuem with an artist friend. When we chanced upon an abstract painting of colors and shapes, I meditated on it for some time and then nudged my friend and asked, "What's it all about?" She told me to study how the reds related to the blues and whites and to one another, what shapes they formed, how these shapes related to other shapes and colors. Following her advice, I began to glimpse the brilliance of the painting.

This passage is much like that painting. In what follows I will explore with you the way the colors and shapes of this passage repeat themselves and relate to one another.

The Basic Message of This Passage

In this passage the author gives us a fine display of his talent for writing exhortatory letters. In verses 5-9 he stresses the positive, that is, the qualifications expected in a church leader and in a Christian in general. In verses 10-16 he underscores the negative: church leaders and Christians in general should avoid the activities of the opponents. (In 2:1-15 he will return to the positive.) I can appreciate the author's style when I recall instructions I received in my years of religious formation. The positive admonition, "The good religious prays daily," was followed by the negative admonition, "Don't pray your breviary while watching a football game on television." The negative example was graphic and brought out a further aspect of the subject under consideration.

By alternating the shapes of positive and negative admonitions, the author is painting a telling picture. In a period marked by transition from the time of Paul to a post-Pauline situation, the church must have structure. By establishing the structure of elders, the church in transition will "amend what was defective" (verse 5). That structure will ensure the teaching of the sound doctrine against opponents (verse 9). But that structure and that teaching of the sound doctrine will only be fruitful if the church is constituted by church leaders and members who lead irreproachable lives. These Christians, unlike the opponents, profess God in word and deed, are respected by all, are obedient, are equipped for every good deed (verse 16, expressed positively).

The Author's Exhortatory Style

In this passage the author alternates between positive admonitions (verse 5-9) and negative ones (verse 10-16) (This same style is in evidence in 2 Tim 2:14-4:8.) By using negative admonitions, the author wants to paint a reverse image of what the model church leader and Christian should be. Let me explain what I mean by taking a closer look at verses 10-16.

Verses 10-16 are a patent example of the author's exhortatory technique of using link-words or catchwords to make his point. I select three examples. First, the author links verse 10 to the preceding verse 6 by the catchword "insubordinate." It makes little difference to him that in verse 6 the "insubordinate" people are children of a candidate for the position of elder whereas in verse 10 the "insubordinates" are the opponents. In either case, insubordination is something to be avoided by Christians and church leaders. Second, we can more readily see the author's use of a link-word in verse 11 if we read "whole *households*" rather than "whole families" (the RSV is not precise here; see 1 Tim 3:15 and 2 Tim 3:6 where the same Greek word, *oikos*, found in Titus 1:11, is translated by "household"). The opponents do not build up households by raising children who are subordinate (verse 6) and by managing households well as "God's stewards" (verse 7), but upset whole households (verse 11). Thirdly, whereas the good Christian and church leader is one who is not greedy for gain (verse 7), the opponent teaches "for base gain" what he has no right to teach (verse 11). As you can see from these three examples, the author is quite artistic in relating the shapes and colors of "subordination," "good household management," and "not greedy" to the positive conduct expected of Christians and to the negative conduct found in the opponents.

Two Problems In This Passage

A. The Relationship Between Elders and Bishops

In verses 5-6 the author embarks on a discussion of the qualities of "elders," but in verse 7 he suddenly changes directions and discusses the qualifications of "a bishop."

Why the shift from "elders" to "a bishop"? While acknowledging other possible explanations, I prefer the following one. The awkwardness of the transition between verses 6 and 7-9 is occasioned by the author's exhortatory style. In 1 Tim 5:17-25 the author commands that the candidates for the position of elder be scrupulously examined, but does not give criteria for that examination. In verse 6 he provides a lean list of qualifications for elders. Apparently that list is the only tradition available to him, and he supplements it with another exhortatory tradition (verses 7-9). He can freely mix traditions about "elders" and "a bishop" because his main concern is that a church in transition have qualified leaders, be they elders or bishops. He links the tradition about elders (verse 6) and the tradition about a bishop (verses 7-9) in three ways. The "for" which begins verse 7 is his first connective. The adjective "blameless" (verses 6 and 7) in his second catchword. The stress on good household management in verses 6 and 7 provides his third link. (The student can profitably examine 1 Tim 6:1-21, which contains two different traditions on wealth (verses 6-10 and 17-19), for a further example of the author's technique of linking together differing traditions.)

In conclusion, the author insists upon structure in the church. Whether that structure be that of a college of elders or of a bishop, the author commands that these leaders have high moral qualifications. The author borrows from different traditions to assemble an adequate listing of the qualifications of an elder. (The interested reader can find additional reflections on the qualifications of church leaders in the commentary on 1 Tim 3:1-13, a passage which embodies a tradition similar to that of Titus 1:7-9).

B. The Teaching of the Opponents

In the commentary on 2 Tim 2:14-26 I note that the author's strictures against the opponents largely serve his exhortatory purpose of painting a picture of conduct to avoid. Therefore, we must read between the lines of exhortation to glean some information about the actual teaching of the opponents. If we undertake such a gleaning operation in this passage, we will discover two things. First, verse 10 ("especially the circumcision party") and verse 14 ("giving heed to Jewish myths") supply additional, but not detailed evidence that the gnostic heresy combatted in the Pastorals had a Jewish component. (See the commentary on 1 Tim 1:3-20 for more detailed information about this Jewish component.) Second, verse 15 provides additional evidence of the ascetic tendencies of the heretics. Their slogan, "To the pure all things are pure" (verse 15), is a misreading of Rom 14:20: "Everything is indeed clean." Misinterpreted Pauline principles like this one led the opponents to their positions of "forbidding marriage and enjoining abstinence from foods" (1 Tim 4:3). Opponents who teach such like should be rebuked by church leaders who "hold firm to the sure word as taught" (verse 9) and who champion the goodness and purity of God's creation.

In resume, the blameless conduct of church leaders and ordinary Christians, adherence to Paul's sound and authoritative teaching as found in these Pastoral Epistles, refutations of those who oppose the sound doctrine, church structure which promotes the development of the Pauline deposit - these are the marks of a church which will succeed in the transition from the age of Paul to a post-Pauline situation.

INCARNATIONAL THEOLOGY.
Titus 2:1-15.

> **2** But as for you, teach what befits sound doctrine. [2]Bid the older men be temperate, serious, sensible, sound in faith, in love, and in steadfastness. [3]Bid the older women likewise to be reverent in behavior, not to be slanderers or slaves to drink; they are to teach what is good, [4]and so train the young women to love their husbands and children, [5]to be sensible, chaste, domestic, kind, and submissive to their husbands, that the word of God may not be discredited. [6]Likewise, urge the younger

men to control themselves. [7]Show yourself in all respects a model of good deeds, and in your teaching show integrity, gravity, [8]and sound speech that cannot be censured, so that an opponent may be put to shame, having nothing evil to say of us. [9]Bid slaves to be submissive to their masters and to give satisfaction in every respect; they are not to be refractory, [10]nor to pilfer, but to show entire and true fidelity, so that in everything they may adorn the doctrine of God our Savior.

[11]For the grace of God has appeared for the salvation of all men, [12]training us to renounce irreligion and worldly passions, and to live sober, upright, and godly lives in this world, [13]awaiting our blessed hope, the appearing of the glory of our great God and Savior Jesus Christ, [14]who gave himself for us to redeem us from all iniquity and to purify for himself a people of his own who are zealous for good deeds.

[15]Declare these things; exhort and reprove with all authority. Let no one disregard you.

A few months ago someone asked me what I was currently working on. I told her that I was writing a commentary on three of the lesser known Pauline epistles, 1-2 Tim and Titus. She paused and then triumphantly remarked, "I know Titus. That's used at Christmas Mass." She was correct, for the second reading for Christmas Midnight Mass is taken from verses 11-14 of this passage. These verses are fitting for Christmas because they invite us to contemplate the new-born babe as God's gracious appearance for our salvation. But these verses, interpreted in the context of the warmth and sentiment of Christmas, can very easily drift away from the moorings of verses 1-10, which contain exhortations about humdrum, daily existence. In what follows I explore the author's thought as he infers the duties of day-in-and-day-out human existence (verses 1-10) from an exalted creed-like statement about the Incarnation (verses 11-14).

The Basic Message of the Passage

Almost from the opening verses of 1 Tim the author of the Pastorals has maintained that Christian existence does not mean withdrawal from the world. In this passage that message comes across loud and clear. Men and women, old and young, are to involve themselves in the ordinary duties of their everyday lives (verses 1-10) and show both non-Christian and heretical opponents that their brand of Christianity leads to morally upright behavior (verses 5, 8,10). The goal of God's salvific grace is not to take Christian men and women out of the world, but to empower them to effectively renounce vice and to lead virtuous lives "in this world" (verses 11-12). Jesus Christ, who involved himself so much in history as to die on a cross, frees his people from all iniquity and instills in them an earnest desire to perform good deeds in this world (verse 14). But such involvement in the stuff of daily life, in imitation of Christ Jesus, does not totally define Christian existence. Christians wait for the appearance of the glory of their God and of their Savior Jesus Christ.

To recapitulate, the author anchors the humdrum and ordinary duties of Christians in the kerygma that God appeared in history in the man Christ Jesus (see 1 Tim 2:5). Christ's deep involvement in human history sets the pattern for his followers, who hope for his appearance and do not possess him now in this world.

The Author's Exhortatory Style in This Passage

The literary finesse of the author's exhortatory style is manifest in this passage. I make five observations on the exhortatory catchwords and connectives he employs.

First, the main catchword which links this passage with chapters 1 and 3 is "good deeds":

1:16	-	"unfit for any *good deed*"
2:7	-	"a model of *good deeds*"
2:14	-	"zealous for *good deeds*"
3:1	-	"ready for every *good deed*" (RSV: "any honest work")

3:8   -   "be careful to apply themselves to *good deeds*"
3:14 -   "let our people learn to apply themselves to *good deeds*"

Unlike the opponents who are "unfit for any good deed," Christians are baptized to be "zealous for good deeds" in this world. (See the commentary on 1 Tim 5:10 for more information on "good deeds" as conduct which promotes human welfare in this world.)

Second, the author uses the catchword "sound" to link this chapter to chapter 1:

1:9   -   "*sound* doctrine"
1:13 -   "that they be *sound* in the faith"
2:1   -   "teach what befits *sound* doctrine"
2:2   -   "*sound* in faith, in love, and in steadfastness"
2:8   -   "and *sound* speech which cannot be censured"

Christian doctrine and the conduct which flows from it do not produce people who are ill and diseased, but ones who are sound and healthy.

Third, note the author's connectives in 2:1. After stressing the positive (1:5-9) and the negative (1:10-16), the author returns to the positive in 2:1-15. In 2:1 he signals his return to the positive by using the connective "but as for you" (see also 1 Tim 6:11; 2 Tim 2:14; 3:10; 4:5). And by means of the catchword "sound doctrine" the author links this positive section to the concluding verse of his previous positive section (1:9).

Fourth, the author's connectives between the traditions of verses 1-10 and 11-14 are visible in the "for" with which he begins verse 11 and in the words "Savior" (verse 10) and "salvation" (verse 11).

Fifth and finally, verse 15 summarizes the previous verses under the rubric of "these things" and prepares for the next section of exhortatory material, 3:1-7. Thus, verse 15 is a bridge between the exhortations of 2:1-14 and those of 3:1-7.

Verses 1-10 Seen By Themselves

When we think about "sound doctrine," we usually think of creeds and other types of abstract formulations. But our author, in his characteristic way, puts exhortations about daily life under the category of "sound doctrine."

In 1 Tim the author patterns his exhortations on a "household" model (see the commentary on 1 Tim 3:14-16 for more detail on this "household" model). Although the author does speak of the duties of one member of the household, the slaves (verses 9-10), his predominant model in this passage is borrowed from a tradition which grouped duties according to sex and age. In the Pastorals the author borrows from various ethical sources in his search for flexible answers to the problems attendant upon churches caught up in the transition from the time of Paul to a post-Pauline situation.

If you came to this passage after having read 1 Tim, you would be struck by the fact that many of the virtues mentioned in this passage are either identical or very similar to those required of church leaders in 1 Tim. For example, both old men (verse 2) and bishops (1 Tim 3:2) are required to be "sensible." The conduct expected of church leaders is the same as that required of ordinary Christians. (See the commentary on 1 Tim 3:1-13 for further discussion of this point.)

In verses 5,8, and 10 we can detect one of the author's principal means of Christianizing secular ethics, namely, his principle of irreproachable conduct. For our purposes I single out verses 4-5 for additional comment: "And so train the young women to love their husbands and children, to be sensible, chaste, domestic, kind, and submissive to their husbands, *that the word of God may not be discredited.*" Because of gnostics who forbade marriage (see 1 Tim 4:3) and because of people's general suspicion of Christians, vicious rumors often circulated about the Christians. The discrediting rumors which the author wants to forestall here may be similar to those refuted by the apologist Theophilus of Antioch:

> They said that our wives are the common property of all and live in promiscuity, that we have intercourse with our own sisters, and - most godless and savage of all - that we partake of human flesh (*Ad Autolycum* 3:4; translation by R. M. Grant; see also Justin Martyr, *Apology* 1.26).

By leading blameless lives, Christian wives will be engaging in the missionary enterprise of showing that "the word of God" promotes the virtues expected of a wife at the time of the Pastorals. (See the commentaries on 1 Tim 2:1-7 and 4:1-16 for an appreciation of the author's position that time-conditioned societal norms are binding on Christians.)

Verses 11-14 Seen By Themselves

Each verse of this section is like a rich vein of gold. I will make a few probes in each verse.

Verse 11 underscores the fact that God's salvation is for all people (see 1 Tim 2:1-7) and that it has appeared in this world.

In verse 12 the author taps into the rich heritage of Greek ethical thought to explain the results of God's involvement in human history. In that thought "training" is the movement from vice to virtue. "Sober, upright, and godly" are shorthand for the cardinal virtues and represent the sum of virtue. God's grace is not mere theoretical training, but effects a real movement from vice to virtue. Because of God's grace Christians, at baptism, renounce irreligion and pursue godliness. Their renunciation of "worldly passions" does not mean withdrawal from the world, for God's grace effects virtuous life "in this world." In sum, God's grace does not inhabit a disembodied soul, but permeates the human life of the Christian. It enables the Christian men and women of the Pastorals to abandon what the wisdom of their time called vice and to warmly embrace what that same wisdom called virtue.

Verse 13 presents us with the very difficult question: Does the author call Jesus Christ "God" here? Grammar alone will not answer the question. I maintain that the author is true to the "low Christology" he espouses throughout the Pastorals and that therefore he does not call Jesus God here. I also call your attention to the other two passages in the Pastorals where the author uses the theological language of "manifestation" and "appearance": 1 Tim 6:14-16 and 2 Tim 1:8-10. Since the author does not call Jesus God in those two parallel passages, I am led to conclude that he does not know him as God in this verse. Perhaps of more importance than this question is the author's emphasis that Christians have a lively hope in the appearing of Jesus Christ. The Christians of the Pastorals have not lost sight of the fact that this world is not the end-all-and-be-all of existence.

Verse 14 begins with an echo of Mk 10:45: "For the Son of man also came not to be served but to serve, and to give his life as a ransom for many" (see also 1 Tim 2:6). After that reminiscence the author moves through three Old Testament passages which supply him with the theological categories to interpret the event of salvation. I italicize the key words in these passages. "And he will *redeem* Israel from all his *iniquities*" (Ps 130:8). "But I will save them from all the backslidings in which they have sinned, and will *cleanse* them; and they shall be *my people*, and I will be their God" (Ez 37:23). "Now, therefore, if you will obey my voice and keep my covenant, you shall be *my own possession* among all peoples" (Ex 19:5).

Two other points call for attention in verse 14. First, the phrase "zealous for good deeds" is without parallel in the Old Testament, and seems to be the author's means of further grounding his theology of salvation. Christians are saved, not for themselves, but to do good deeds in this world. Second, the Hellenistic "appearance" language of verses 11 and 13, especially if read in the context of the merry and confident mood of Christmas, might give the impression that God is easily accessible to the eyes of faith.

Verse 14 soberly corrects this impression. God's appearance is about as easily discernible to the eyes of faith as it was in the suffering of Jesus Christ who "gave himself for us." When God appears in the ordinariness of daily marital fidelity and love, in the darkness of doubt and depression, in the suffering of terminal cancer, in the crisis of martyrdom (see 2 Tim), it is not easy to see him. We stand ready to shout out paeans of praise to our God for his goodness in creation, incarnation, and salvation. Often, however, it takes weeks and months of stumbling in the dark before we discover how the God we so want to praise has appeared in our lives. And then we may find him in the pots and pans and runny noses of our daily existence, and not in some spectacular event or miracle which is discontinuous with the commitments which make up the routine of our daily lives. Perhaps, the following analogy will explain my point. A mother's act of saving her children from a burning building is heroic and spectacular, but not discontinuous with her daily commitments to them. That heroic act must be seen against the backdrop of her daily self-sacrificing for them.

Incarnational Theology: The Connections
Between Verses 1-10 and 11-14

In the preceding paragraphs we have seen that, on the one hand, the author does not merely juxtapose verses 1-10 and 11-14. On the other hand, he does not extensively explore their interrelationships or address himself to our contemporary concerns of the time-conditioned nature of norms and of institutional evil. But it does seem clear why he connects these two sets of verses.

Christian existence means the affirmation that our Savior has appeared in history as a human being, Christ Jesus (verses 11-14). Because of that prior affirmation, Christians affirm human institutions, which define and prescribe their daily lives in this world, and purpose to lead a life of virtue within the parameters of these institutions (verses 1-10). Christian existence is not body-less and time-less, but life in a world of structures and covenants. In his accentuation of the realness of God's appearance for the salvation of all people, the author avoids the senti- mentality often associated with the Incarnation. The babe in the manger does grow up, lead a full human life, and is crucified. God's grace trains Christians to fashion the fabric of their daily lives from commitments to one another. They do not affirm the goodness of human life and of God's creation blindly. The joy of Christmas mingles with the obscurity and pain of Calvary. There are those "worldly passions," which gnaw at their allegiance to Jesus Christ. There is that moment of martyrdom when they, like Paul, anguish and struggle before giving up this life to "take hold of the life which is life indeed" (1 Tim 6:19).

GOD'S GENEROSITY AS A MODEL FOR CHRISTIANS.
Titus 3:1-15.

3 Remind them to be submissive to rulers and authori- ties, to be obedient, to be ready for any honest work, [2]to speak evil of no one, to avoid quarreling, to be gentle, and to show perfect courtesy toward all men. [3]For we ourselves were once foolish, disobedient, led astray, slaves to various passions and pleasures, passing our days in malice and envy, hated by men and hating one another; [4]but when the goodness and loving kindness of God our Savior appeared, [5]he saved us, not because of deeds done by us in righteousness, but in virtue of his own mercy, by the washing of regeneration and renewal in the Holy Spirit, [6]which he poured out upon us richly through Jesus Christ our Savior, [7]so that we might be justified by his grace and become heirs in hope of eternal life. [8]The saying is sure.

I desire you to insist on these things, so that those who have believed in God may be careful to apply themselves to good deeds; these are excellent and profitable to men. [9]But avoid stupid controversies, genealogies, dissensions, and quarrels over the law, for they are unprofitable and futile. ¹⁰As for a man who is factious, after admonishing him once or twice, have nothing more to do with him, ¹¹knowing that such a person is perverted and sinful; he is self-condemned.

¹²When I send Artemas or Tychicus to you, do your best to come to me at Nicopolis, for I have decided to spend the winter there. ¹³Do your best to speed Zenas the lawyer and Apollos on their way; see that they lack nothing. ¹⁴And let our people learn to apply themselves to good deeds, so as to help cases of urgent need, and not to be unfruitful.

¹⁵All who are with me send greetings to you. Greet those who love us in the faith.

Grace be with you all.

Let me begin this section by asking you a question: What is your idea of God? Is God all-powerful? All-good? All-just? Father? Mother? In this section the author gives his answer to that question. For him God is good and benevolent and wills life, goodness, and salvation for all people. The author even goes further and demands that we, his readers, imitate God in his generosity and love for all humankind. In what follows we look at the structure of the author's answer and demand from different perspectives.

The Author's Basic Message

To help us appreciate the author's rich message here, allow me to outline his sequence of thought. You will readily note how the author uses the catchword "good deeds" to link his thought together:

3:1-2 - "Remind them" (see 2 Tim 2:14) introduces new exhortations for all Christians, e.g., "be ready for every *good deed*" (RSV: "for any honest work")

3:3-7   -   Motivation for these new exhortations is rooted in a "then/now" schema which is introduced by "for." Although Christians were wretches *then* (verse 3), God has *now* lavished his goodness and loving kindness upon them (verses 4-7).

3:8   -   Because the God they experience in baptism is gracious, Christians should be gracious and apply themselves to *good deeds* to benefit others (see verse 14). These good deeds are *profitable.*

3:9   -   Controversies, etc., are *unprofitable.*

3:10-11 -   Instructions on how to deal with those who engage in such *unprofitable* matters as genealogies.

3:12   -   "*do your best*" - Paul's situation and concluding remarks.

3:13   -   "*do your best*" - be gracious to Zenas and Apollos

3:14   -   our people "apply themselves to *good deeds*" like the supplying of the needs of Zenas and Apollos (see verse 8).

3:15   -   This letter is to be read by all.

Christians should live a harmonious, generous, and gracious life with all their fellow men and women (verses 1-2). The rationale for these admonitions is this: Because God has shown his gracious love for us, unworthy sinners as we were, we should imitate God and love our fellow human beings gratuitously (verses 3-7). And because we have experienced God as such a lavish benefactor, we should do good deeds for others, with no strings attached (verse 8). (Seen from this perspective, the translation "good deeds" is more accurate than "honest work/occupations," for it corresponds to the author's thought here and to his use of the phrase "good deeds" in other passages.)

Verses 4-7 Seen By Themselves

I single out these verses for separate treatment because of their own signal importance and to help preachers who may want to base their sermon on this, the second reading for Christmas Mass at Dawn in the Roman Catholic lectionary.

The "then/now" schema. Verses 4-7 form the "now" part of the "then/now" sequence of verses 3-7, a sequence which is evidenced in one of its simplest forms in Eph 5:8: "For *once* you were darkness, but *now* you are light in the Lord; walk as children of light." As with all "then/now" schemas we can ask: What event caused the movement from "then" to "now"? The event which caused that transformation is baptism: "the washing of regeneration and renewal in the Holy Spirit." Because they have experienced God's goodness, loving kindness, and mercy in baptism, Christians know that they have moved out of the "then" of a morally wretched life into a "now" where the doing of "good deeds" is in grateful response to mercy received.

This passage boasts of liturgical language. The first clue to its presence is the use of "we/us/our" rather than "you." The author drops the exhortatory style of "you," and quotes from materials which describe what happened to all Christians. The second clue is the frequency of exalted language: goodness and loving kindness, deeds done by us in righteousness, washing of regeneration, etc. Verse 8 provides a final clue by marking these verses off as a fixed or "sure saying."

Is this passage Pauline? While acknowledging that many of the terms found here are not used by Paul (e.g., washing of regeneration), there is sufficient evidence to call this passage Pauline. I marshal the evidence of "deeds done by us in righteousness" and "justified by his grace" (see Rom 5:1 and the commentary on 2 Tim 1:6-14). These expressions are tell-tale signs that this passage belongs to the Pauline family. As an analogy, I invite you to recall the familiar reaction one has when meeting the various members of a family: "Jack looks different from Mike and Sue from Maryanne, but there's a family resemblance which says they're all O'Hara's." The Pauline elements we find in verses 4-7 are different from those we might find in Romans, but there is sufficient family resemblance to call them Pauline.

The words "goodness and loving kindness" have their origin in Hellenistic benefactor language. As a matter of fact, the Greek behind "loving kindness" literally means "philanthropy." God has loved humans so much that he saved them from vice and gave them the gift of a life of doing good deeds. And God acted so "through Jesus Christ our Savior."

The Author's Flexible Approach to Christian Life

Throughout the commentary on 1 Tim and Titus I have directed your attention to the author's flexible approach to church order. That is, while he desires structure in churches which call themselves Pauline, he does not insist on one particular structure, for example, a college of elders or a bishop. The admonitions of Titus 2:1-10 and 3:1-2 are not exhaustive listings of conduct expected of Christians, for the author does not see fit to "legislate" every detail of Christian conduct. In verse 8 he gives a blanket principle, allowing for personal responsibility and communal discernment: "I desire you to insist on these things, so that those who have believed in God may be careful to apply themselves to good deeds." Christians should do whatever they discern "good deeds" to be.

From Liturgy To Life

For some ten years now a motto has been circulating in my Franciscan Order: "From paper to life." If we Franciscans are to be renewed according to the spirit of Vatican II, then we have to put into practice our constitutions of renewal; we must move from paper to life. Titus 3:4-7 is yet another example of our author's intention to move from liturgy to life. (See also 1 Tim 1:15; 2:4-6; 3:16; 6:12-16; 2 Tim 1:8-10; 2:8-13; Titus 2:11-14.) The creeds which the

Christians of the Pastorals profess and the hymns which they sing must not be filed away in the sacristy until the next liturgy. They must enter into the mainstream of daily life. It seems that the author knows the exaltation and exhilaration of liturgy splendidly celebrated. He knows the powerful presence of the Lord who is worshipped at liturgy with creeds and hymns. But he insists that liturgy begets daily Christian life. Reflecting on the liturgical traditions of verses 4-7, he resolves to imitate God's goodness and benevolence in his daily life. Let us enter into the author's reflections and imitate our all-good and gracious God in the ordinariness of marketplace, home, and school. In our daily lives let us continue our worship of the God of life and love.

ANNOTATED READING LIST

Barrett, C. K., "Pauline Controversies in the Post-Pauline Period," *New Testament Studies* 20 (1973/74), pp. 229-245.

A brilliant article on the diverse images of Paul which vied with one another in the late first century and second century. It is probable that it was only through the Pastorals' understanding of Paul that the genuine epistles of the radical Paul were accepted into the canon of the New Testament.

_____, *The Pastoral Epistles*, New Clarendon Bible; Oxford: Clarendon Press, 1963.

Balanced and clear presentation of Pauline and non-Pauline character of the Pastorals. He makes a telling point for any commentator's examination of conscience: "Students have too often approached the Pastorals with the (perhaps unconscious) assumption that given the opportunity they could have written the Epistles very much better themselves" (p. 34).

Dibelius, Martin; Conzelmann, Hans, *The Pastoral Epistles: A Commentary on the Pastoral Epistles*. Hermeneia; Philadelphia: Fortress, 1972.

Very rich in non-biblical parallels. Has the Greek text with English translation in brackets.

Fuller, Reginald H., "The Pastoral Epistles" in J. Paul Sampley, Joseph Burgess, Gerhard Krodel, Reginald Fuller, *Ephesians, Colossians, 2 Thessalonians, The Pastoral Epistles*. Proclamation Commentaries; Philadelphia: Fortress, 1978, pp. 97-121.

A very clear summary of years of reflection on the nature of these epistles.

Houlden, J. L. *The Pastoral Epistles: I and II Timothy, Titus.* The Pelican New Testament Commentaries; Harmondswirth, England: Penguin, 1976.

A very readable and provocative commentary from which I have benefited much.

Käsemann, Ernst, *Jesus Means Freedom.* Philadelphia: Fortress, 1969, pp. 85-100.

, "Paul and Early Catholicism," *New Testament Questions of Today.* Philadelphia: Fortress, 1969, pp. 236-251.

Käsemann has the gift of sharply formulating issues. His provocative hypothesis is that the Pastorals are a New Testament example of what later came to be called Catholicism. This hypothesis, although helpful for many years, needs a thorough overhaul.

Karris, Robert J., "The Background and Significance of the Polemic of the Pastoral Epistles," *Journal of Biblical Literature* 92 (1973), pp. 549-564.

In this periodical article I give detailed evidence for the stereotyped nature of the polemic of the Pastorals. In this commentary I modify my interpretation of how the author of the Pastorals employs this stereotyped polemic.

Kelly, J. N. D., *A Commentary on the Pastoral Epistles: I Timothy, II Timothy, Titus.* Black's New Testament Commentaries; London: Adam & Charles Black, 1963.

One of the great strengths of this commentary is the author's pursuit and detection of the sequence of thought in the Pastorals.